Yorkshire

Car Tours

John Brooks

Acknowledgements

My thanks go to Josh Brooks who was an invaluable map-reader,
and to Heather Pearson and Sandy Sims at the Ordnance Survey for
painstakingly checking the text against the maps. I am very grateful
to all of them for their support.

Front cover photograph: *Kettlewell*
Title page photograph: *Staithes*

Author: John Brooks
Series Editor: Anne-Marie Edwards
Editor: Paula Granados
Designers: Brian Skinner, Doug Whitworth
Photographs: Jarrold Publishing

Ordnance Survey   ISBN 0-3190-0493-7
Jarrold Publishing   ISBN 0-7117-0826-6

First published 1995 by Ordnance Survey and Jarrold Publishing

Ordnance Survey   Jarrold Publishing
Romsey Road   Whitefriars
Maybush   Norwich NR3 1TR
Southampton SO16 4GU

© Ordnance Survey and Jarrold Publishing 1995
Maps © Crown copyright 1995

Printed in Great Britain by Jarrold Printing, Norwich. 1/95

CONTENTS

3

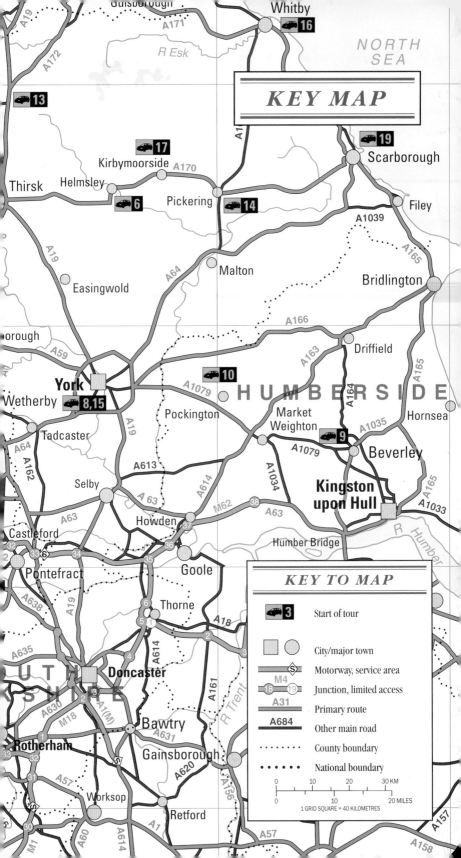

AN INTRODUCTION
TO YORKSHIRE

At home and abroad Yorkshire is known for its pudding, traditionally served on its own before the meat, an uncomplicated mixture of flour, eggs and milk which, if made by a skilled hand, is delicious. A Yorkshireman's character is noted for being equally straightforward and wholesome. He (or, of course, she) is said to be noted for his plain-speaking, his warm heart, his stubbornness, and for the great care he takes of his 'brass' – the money in his pocket. It is said that he is also intensely loyal both to his friends and to his native county. These characteristics seem to be found all over the vast county which has retained its cohesion and character in spite of all efforts made to rationalise or divide it.

Traditionally Yorkshire, always England's largest county, was divided into three Ridings from the Danish 'thriday' or 'third part' – West, North and East. The West Riding on its own was bigger than any other English shire until the boundaries of all the counties were changed in 1974. The most hurtful of these adjustments to a Yorkshireman was the loss of the East Riding to the new county of Humberside. Happily, most of these wrongs seem about to be put right, though it is unlikely that the term 'Riding' will be revived.

This book of car tours deals mainly with those parts that have always been popular with tourists – the Yorkshire Dales and the North Yorkshire Moors. In addition, there are routes which explore lesser-known countryside like the Wolds, the valley of the River Ouse, and the centre of the county around Holmfirth, a town which achieved fame through being the setting for the long-running television series *Last of the Summer Wine*.

Environment must affect the personality of people through the generations. If it places harsh demands on settlers then they invariably take on different characteristics from neighbours who have had to battle less fiercely for their livelihoods. In Yorkshire much of the terrain was demanding and, from the earliest times, settlers had to defend their land from incomers seeking to take over fields and townships laboriously cleared of the forest which then covered nearly the whole of Yorkshire.

The Roman occupation had little effect on

Skidby Mill is a landmark in the flat landscape south of Beverley

Springtime in Wensleydale

the primitive herdspeople living in the Dales and on the Moors, but their roads crossed the Pennines and were guarded by small forts, while York and Malton had more substantial garrisons. When Roman influence waned after the fifth century and the Dark Ages set in, successive waves of settlers came from Europe, pillaging villages and setting up their own communities. The Angles came first from Germany and southern Denmark. As well as keeping livestock they grew crops and liked to live in villages. In contrast, the Norse invaders who succeeded them brought the pastoral way of life they had followed in Scandinavia. They lived in small family units and moved their cattle to upland pastures in summer, often living in summer houses close to their herds. In winter the family moved to lower ground and shared their homestead with their beasts. In some of the more remote dales this way of life survived until the nineteenth century, and place names ending in 'sett' reveal where they had their summer homes. Much upland terminology also derives from the Norse settlers – words like gill, rigg and tarn – and it is said that Norwegians recognise the cadences of the Dalesman's speech today.

The Normans proved to be the most unwelcome invaders. Faced with stubborn resistance in the north of his new realm, William I set about devastating the northern counties. During his campaign, known as 'The Harrowing of the North', a quarter of the population died, either being slain by the conquerors or dying of starvation.

William's supporters were given grants of land and erected castles to protect them. They also began to endow monasteries, and these had an ever-increasing influence on the economy of Yorkshire until they were disbanded by Henry VIII after 1537. This action released an enormous amount of land into private ownership and soon lead to the creation of a new class of citizen, especially prevalent in Yorkshire, the yeoman farmer. His successors today have inherited the resilience and sturdy independence of spirit that is the result of countless centuries of strife and hardship.

The Yorkshire Dales

Geologists know the Dales as the region of Britain which best displays the characteristics of 'karst' scenery (it takes its name from a part of Yugoslavia where similar outcrops of limestone are found). This is due to the rock known as Great Scar Limestone which is to be found in the southern dales. The rock is composed of the shells of sea creatures which died three hundred million years ago. They lived in the calm tropical sea which covered the region for several million years and their shells gradually built up into a deep layer of soft, chalky rock. More turbulent times followed and shales, sandstones and gritstones were washed down into the sea to cover and compact the shells. Under compression they became metamorphosed into hard rock 640 feet (195 m) deep. Later earth movements raised this up into a gigantic dome, still capped by the other sedimentary rocks.

Many more millions of years passed and gradually water, made slightly acid by the carbon dioxide in the air, began to eat into the weaknesses in the limestone. Streams flowed off the impervious rocks on the upper slopes of the hills into fissures made by rainwater

*Brimham Rocks
These outcrops of
millstone grit have
been weathered into
weird shapes*

and began to exploit horizontal cracks, thus making cave systems. Sometimes these collapsed leaving massive gorges. More recently, in geological terms, Ice Age glaciers flowed down valleys originally made by stream water, ripping out their sides to make the broad 'U-shaped' valleys so characteristic of the Dales. Meanwhile, underneath the surface, drops of lime-rich water fell from the ceilings of caves to build up into the fantastic formations which are to be seen today in the various 'show caves'.

One of the distinctive features which newcomers will notice in the upper Dales are the innumerable field barns (known as laithes) which are dotted about the landscape. Until the Second World War cattle were kept inside them in the winter with a supply of hay from the neighbouring feeds. Throughout the winter months the farmer had to walk round his laithes to feed and milk his stock. These days they are seldom used for animals, unless it is to shelter ewes and their offspring at lambing.

*The romantic ruin
of Barden Tower in
Wharfedale*

The North Yorkshire Moors

The whole area experienced violent earth movements about eighty million years ago when the 'Cleveland Dome' was suddenly thrust up from the bed of the ocean. It is composed mainly of shales and sandstones, though there are outcrops of limestone to the south where the moors give way to the Hambleton Hills. However, this rock differs from the dazzling-white limestone found in the Dales. The limestone of the Hambleton Hills is akin to that of the Cotswolds and is a favourite building material in these parts.

Typical red-roofed cottages at Helmsley

Thus, many of the villages here look as though they have been transposed from Gloucestershire, their buildings being of similar honey-coloured stone. To make the comparison even more complete they frequently have sparkling streams running through them. To the north the ill-drained sandstones and shales are covered with a thin layer of peaty topsoil on which heather thrives, the largest expanse of open heather moorland to be found in England, and which is

ENJOY YOUR TOUR

Please read through the tour before starting, and if visibility is poor when you intend to set out reject those offering fine panoramas from lofty viewpoints. Hopefully, you will find a neighbouring route which visits historic buildings or towns. Note that all routes are circular so they can be started at any point. Tour instructions are in bold. There are also boxed letters which tie in with those on the map. Their purpose is to aid your navigation and, in many instances, highlight sections of the route requiring particular attention. The times given for each tour cover motoring only but, if you decide to explore footpaths or visit attractions, then they can easily take the best part of a day. It is possible that opening times of the various attractions may have changed, and it is advisable to telephone before visiting. If you plan more extensive walks the Pathfinder guides or Pathfinder maps at 1:25 000 (2½ inches to 1 mile/4 cm to 1 km) are ideal – for details see inside back cover.

In order to see some of the loveliest areas in Yorkshire many of the routes here include narrow roads with steep gradients. Some pass through fords which are usually easy to cross, though it might be hazardous to attempt them after exceptional rainfall. Obviously, driving on lesser roads in semi-mountainous countryside presents problems not encountered elsewhere on highways. It is always best to anticipate there being a milk tanker or kamikaze delivery van approaching blind corners from the opposite direction! Never trust roadside sheep who may look preoccupied with their nibbling – they are just as likely to amble in front of traffic. And finally, if you are sightseeing on a single-track road, pull over as often as possible to allow following traffic to pass.

glorious in late summer. This is the habitat favoured by grouse, curlew and merlin, the latter a very rare predator.

Over the millennia since the violent creation of the Dome the massif has been weathered into the shape seen today. Swift streams have cut valleys into its rock, and here they generally run on a north-south axis rather than the west-east of the Dales. Glaciation also played its part in modelling the landscape, gouging out steep-sided valleys and creating spectacular features such as the Hole of Horcum, an enormous natural amphitheatre (see Tour 14).

Much of the sandstone is rich in iron, and this lead to intensive mining on the top of the moor from the seventeenth century until the 1930s. Today it is hard to imagine the tops of the moors being noisy and smoky with industry for this is a favourite place with people seeking beauty and solitude. Although you can drive up to many of the beauty spots you have to leave the car to capture the true essence of this wonderful countryside.

The Vales and the Wolds

Yorkshire's two vales, those of York and Pickering, are broad plains which provide some of the best agricultural land in the north of

The Old Silent Inn at Stanbury, West Yorkshire, the haunt of a former landlady

England. Both owe their origin to the action of glaciers and Pickering once stood close to a large glacial lake. The rivers which run through the vales follow strange courses, dictated by the deposits of mud and rock left by the glaciers when they melted at the end of the Ice Age. Individual boulders were carried great distances in the ice flows, some in the Vale of Pickering coming from southern Norway.

The Vale of York was covered with an almost impenetrable oak forest until medieval times, and was a popular hunting-ground with nobility and royalty in the Middle Ages. By the eighteenth century the forest had been cleared and the land drained to make the rich acres that are farmed so successfully today. Many large estates are situated in the vale, often surrounded by villages specially built by their proprietors. Castle Howard is by far the grandest of these, standing on the edge of the vale amongst the Howardian Hills which took their name from the family which built the mansion.

The Wolds are the northern extremity of chalk uplands which extend southwards down the eastern side of England to end in the South Downs on the Channel coast. Chalk has the same composition as limestone, but has not been subjected to heat and pressure in the same way. Thus, it remains porous, but is a much softer bedrock giving a gentle landscape often reminiscent of Sussex. The fields are large here and on the whole hedgeless, but on good days the vistas are superb, and the back roads mainly used in

The lovely landscape of Esk Dale – Littlebeck near Whitby

this book are seldom busy. Prehistoric settlers enjoyed living on the wolds as they found the land easy to clear – signs of this early occupation are plain to see. Much later medieval peasants were cleared from the wolds by landowners to make way for sheep, and

many villages were abandoned at this time. Wharram Percy is the most evocative of these, a hidden place where beauty is mixed with a degree of sadness.

York

The city has seen more than two thousand years of continuous habitation which commenced when the Romans established a fort named Eboracum in the first century. They chose a strategically-important site – at that time the River Ouse was tidal up to

Pen-y-ghent overlooks Ribblesdale

this point, where it is joined by the little River Foss. The Roman settlement grew quickly into an important outpost of their empire. It covered more than fifty acres when they were at the height of their power, which lasted for nearly four hundred years. In the year 866 the Vikings captured York and began another important phase of the city's history. They called it Jorvik, and it grew to be the capital of their empire, albeit one made largely of wood. Two hundred years later the Normans came and, after stout resistance by the Anglo-Danes, stabilised the region by their policy of 'Harrowing the North' which left the city and surrounding area barren and desolate. William I built two castles to protect the city and made this his administration centre. A large Norman church was built, its crypt surviving beneath the sanctuary of the present minster.

The minster was begun in 1291 and completed c. 1350. The word minster comes from the Saxon and means a centre for evangelism. York Minster is the largest Gothic cathedral north of the Alps and dominates the city both physically and spiritually. Its medieval glass is outstanding, the great west window has tracery following the shape of a heart and has the nickname 'the heart of Yorkshire', and the transepts have the wonderful Rose Window as well as the fifty-foot lancets known as 'The Five Sisters', a masterpiece of medieval design.

York has many more splendours – the Shambles is a picturesque medieval street, there are the walls and gates dating from the same time as well as many fine Georgian buildings. Furthermore, York is a city which continues to flourish, it has a host of fine shops and tourist attractions ranging from the enthralling National Railway Museum to the re-creation of the Viking city, Jorvik, complete with sounds and smells. Tours 8 and 15 commence in York for those wanting to explore this fine city.

RIBBLESDALE, LITTONDALE AND PEN-Y-GHENT

60 MILES – 3 HOURS
START AND FINISH AT INGLETON

This figure-of-eight route passes through the most dramatic limestone countryside to be found in Yorkshire, and also follows part of the Settle-Carlisle railway up to its spectacular crossing of Ribblesdale over the Ribble Head viaduct. Walkers will enjoy the opportunity of climbing Pen-y-ghent, Ingleborough or Whernside, or making the less energetic excursion to the Ingleton waterfalls. The configuration of the route means that it can be separated into two shorter tours if preferred.

Turn left out of Ingleton's Tourist Information Centre car park on to the B6255 (the road to Hawes). Pass the police station on the right then, almost immediately, turn right towards Clapham. This pleasant roller-coaster road is very twisty and climbs much of the time. There are good views to the right towards the Forest of Bowland. A layby to the right, just before a 1-in-7 gradient, provides a good viewpoint with the village of Clapham below.

Turn left into Clapham at a T-junction when the road meets the B6480. Cross the bridge and turn left into the car park by the National Park Information Centre. You can walk to Ingleborough Cave from here (either through the Reginald Farrer Nature Reserve or by public bridleway). Visitors are able to see many of the most exciting features of the 5-mile system, including the Hall of Reflections, Pillar Hall and Long Gallery, in a guided tour which takes about an hour. There is no

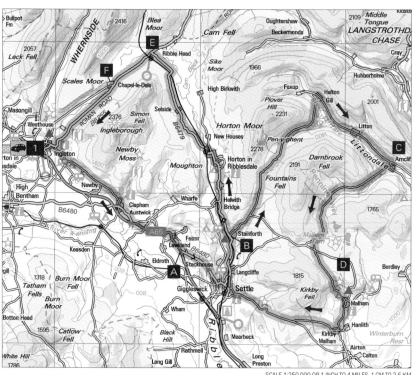

SCALE 1:250 000 OR 1 INCH TO 4 MILES 1 CM TO 2.5 KM

The scenery around Arncliffe gave Kingsley inspiration when he wrote The Water Babies

vehicular access to the cave.

Pass the New Inn on the left to leave the village. When you meet the A65 (just over 5 miles from Ingleton) turn left towards Settle. Carry on for 3 miles to pass the Yorkshire Dales Falconry Centre. About ½ mile past the centre turn left A towards Settle on to the B6480. There is a fine view of the fells surrounding the town before the road drops down steeply.

Giggleswick, the village before Settle, has a magnificent parish church as well as a famous public school. **Descend past the swimming-pool and over a bridge into Settle. Turn left immediately after the bridge on to the B6479 towards Horton in Ribblesdale. The Settle-Carlisle railway is on the right and the Watershead Mill Craft Centre on the left. Go past the hamlet of Langcliffe and up the pleasant green valley of Ribblesdale to the picturesque village of Stainforth.** Its name derives from the feature which gave the village its *raison d'être* – the 'stony ford' across the River Ribble which was part of the ancient trading route between

---

• PLACES OF INTEREST •

The Settle-Carlisle Railway
The Midland Railway Company undertook the construction of this line in order to extend their services northwards into Scotland. The route crossed exceptionally rugged terrain, and the engineering problems were formidable, entailing the building of 325 bridges, 21 viaducts and 14 tunnels in its 72 miles. Its highest point at 1,169 feet (356 m) is at Aisgill at the head of the Eden valley. In the past there must have been many a fireman who sighed with relief at reaching this point without suffering the indignity of coming to a halt through lack of steam. The line was completed in 1875, about 5,000 navvies having been engaged in the work. Accidents claimed the lives of many of them, especially in the building of the Ribblehead viaduct, the most spectacular of the engineering works which has 24 arches, the tallest being 105 feet high.

Today the Settle-Carlisle is a mecca for railway enthusiasts. It is supported by the National Park and local authorities who recognise its importance not only historically but also as an asset to tourism. Many of the stations are situated in remote areas of moorland and walkers enjoy using them as starting points.

Settle
Market day here is on Tuesday when the town is thronged with Dalespeople bustling around the array of colourful stalls.

The town's charter dates from 1249, but it is its seventeenth- and eighteenth-century buildings which give Settle its appeal. The Shambles, which are Victorian cottages built above a Georgian arcade, overlook the market square and are typical of the town's idiosyncratic architecture.

Settle is an excellent centre from which to explore Ribblesdale and Craven.

The Museum of North Craven Life. This museum occupies a seventeenth-century building in Chapel Street. Telephone: (01729) 822854.

The Three Peaks

This is the name given to the highland area centred on Ingleton and bounded by three formidable Pennine summits – Whernside (2,416 feet/736 metres), Ingleborough (2,376 feet/724 metres), and Pen-y-ghent (2,278 feet/694 metres). There are some people who can climb all three in a single day, but ordinary folk should be warned against tackling any one of them unless they are equipped with good boots, warm clothing, emergency rations, maps and compass.

Ingleton

The coming of the railway brought tourists to a small town previously known only for its market. Ingleton capitalised on this by promoting its famous Falls Walk, a path which follows the River Twiss up to Thornton Force through a valley which becomes a ravine as it nears the falls. The return is via the equally beautiful valley of the River Doe. A small charge is made for entry to the paths, but is worthwhile, especially after heavy rain.

Yorkshire Dales Falconry Centre

Visitors will see birds of prey from all over the world, many of them in flight as there are regular flying demonstrations. Refreshments.

Open throughout the year except Christmas Day. Situated 2 miles west of Settle on A65. Telephone: (01729) 825164.

White Scar Cave

This is the largest show cave in England, and visitors walk 1/2 mile into the hillside, passing beneath waterfalls and seeing a wide variety of geological formations. White Scar is 1 1/2 miles from Ingleton on the B6255 road to Hawes. Café and picnic area. Telephone: (015242) 41244.

Ingleborough Cave

There is no vehicular access to the cave. The walk up to its mouth takes about half an hour from Clapham. However, visitors are rewarded with a wonderful array of formations, the cave corals being particularly famous.

Open daily March–October. Weekends only during winter. Telephone: (015242) 51242.

Lancaster and York. In the seventeenth century a graceful bridge was built over the river, and this may be crossed on foot to reach the lovely waterfalls below.

Turn right B at the car park and toilets into the village following the signs to Halton Gill and Arncliffe. Turn left at the T-junction on to a lane which climbs steadily. Keep ahead ignoring the turning to Malham on the right. As you approach the lower slopes of Pen-y-ghent on the left you will see that its whale-back shape increasingly dominates the skyline. There are parking spaces by the open road after Dale Head, where the Pennine Way crosses the road. Its summit is at a height of 2,277 feet (694 m), and the energetic may wish to climb to

this from here.

This is a gated road and the gate may be closed against you a little further on before the road begins to descend. A high wall to the right hides a wonderful view of the precipitous valley, and there are even more spectacular views of Littondale ahead.

Halton Gill nestles in the bottom of the valley with a little bridge in the foreground. **At the T-junction turn right towards Litton and Arncliffe.** You are now heading down Littondale, with the River Skirfare to the right, though this may be dry in the summer. This part of the route is delightful and Litton, the upper village of Littondale, is most charming with its stone cottages.

Arncliffe C, the next

village, is where the route changes direction. Turn right to cross the bridge and pass the church. Bear right again on to the road signposted to Malham and continue past the wide green. At the end of Arncliffe you will find a tearoom in Raikes Cottage.

Now head south-westwards up a very steep valley, again on a gated road. The drop to the left is almost vertical, and the road twists around hairpin bends descending steeply to cross Darnbrook Beck. It is the few barns and cottages, like those at Darnbrook, which give scale to this magnificent landscape. A sign by a cattle-grid informs travellers that they are on Malham Tarn National Trust property and, soon after, the route crosses the Pennine Way again, this time at Tennant Gill. **Keep ahead when a drive leaves to the left to the Malham Field Centre, but fork left 1/2 mile further on when the road divides to head towards Malham. Continue straight over the crossroads which follows. (Turn left if you wish to see the Malham Tarn Nature Reserve.)**

The views are wonderful from here with an amazing amount of exposed rock. Malham Cove D is to the left, although it is impossible to see from the car. It is best to explore this famous natural amphitheatre, with a backdrop of sheer cliffs 300 feet (91 m) high, by walking up from Malham village. The descent into Malham is very steep and the Pennine Way joins the road just before the village.

The National Park Information Centre is situated in Malham, as is a rescue post for climbers and cavers. There are two car parks in Malham, the first on the left and the second on the far side of the village.

Follow the road out of the village to come to Kirkby Malham and, when the road to Skipton bends sharply to the left, take the one ahead

to Settle. The road climbs out of the village through an avenue of hawthorn and beech trees. **At a T-junction on the open moor bear right to Settle.** The hills which overlook Settle from the west are more jagged than those seen earlier. The waterfall at Scaleber is impressive after wet weather. The road passes over a bridge and then below the steep Sugar Loaf Hill which overlooks Settle from the east. There is a descending gradient of 1-in-5 here. **Turn right at the T-junction to bring you back to the main street.**

Leave Settle, as before, on the B6479 to Horton in Ribblesdale. However, this time keep on the main road past Stainforth. The road climbs steadily up Ribblesdale, and the limestone escarpments become increasingly obvious as you travel northwards. As you approach Horton in Ribblesdale, Ingleborough may be seen to the left and Pen-y-ghent to the right. The road crosses the river at the village, which has pubs, a café, car park and toilets, and then resumes its north-westerly course closely following the Settle-Carlisle railway – this is

The village of Giggleswick snug beneath the hills which surround it

a favourite venue for steam locomotive enthusiasts. As the road approaches Ribble Head the scenery becomes even more spectacular. **When the B6479 meets the Ingleton to Hawes road at Ribble Head E, turn left along the B6255 to start the last leg of the tour back to Ingleton.**

There is a wonderful view of the Ribblehead viaduct just as you make the turn. **Pass the Station Inn and go below the railway once more.** Pause a little further on to look back at another aspect of the viaduct. **After another 3 miles, just beyond the Old**

Hill Inn, there is a byway to the right which is an alternative way back to Ingleton. It passes the tiny church at Chapel-le-Dale **F** which has touching monuments to those killed in the construction of the railway.

Otherwise, keep on the main road (B6255) to pass below Raven Scar. This is a steep escarpment on the north-western flank of Ingleborough. Two miles before reaching Ingleton you pass White Scar Cave on the left, one of the most spectacular show caverns of the Dales. ■

The distinctive shape of Ingleborough, one of the Three Peaks

SWALEDALE AND WENSLEYDALE WITH CASTLE BOLTON AND SEMER WATER

41 MILES – 2½ HOURS
START AND FINISH AT HAWES

This tour takes you along lanes giving access to some of the most outstanding vistas in Swaledale and Wensleydale. The route passes through famous dales villages and visits Castle Bolton as well as the Butter Tubs and Aysgarth Falls. Those drivers nervous of narrow lanes and steep gradients might be advised to ignore the diversions to Ivelet Bridge (after ◼B *) and Semer Water (after* ◼E *).*

Turn right out of the Dales Countryside Museum car park at Hawes and bear right round the traffic island to cross the one-way system, taking the road ahead to Muker. Pass Hawes Rural Workshops on the left and cross the bridge over the River Ure. This is a beautiful part of Wensleydale, with numerous footpaths winding across the meadows, one of them being the Pennine Way. The riverside pastures are brilliant with buttercups in early summer.

At the T-junction after the bridge turn left towards Hardraw. The waterfall here, Hardraw Force, is the highest single-leap waterfall in England with a drop of more than 96 feet (29 m). **To visit Hardraw Force it is best to keep straight along this road into the village.** The footpath to the falls is over private ground, and you have to pay a small charge at the Green Dragon Inn in order to use it.

If you do not wish to **visit the waterfall turn right 200 yards (183 m) after the T-junction, following the signs to 'Muker via Butter Tubs'.** The road climbs past a

---

• PLACES OF INTEREST •

Hawes
Hawes stands at the head of Wensleydale and is a busy market town as well as being a favourite centre for tourists and walkers – it is the mid-point of the Pennine Way. Both of its traditional industries, rope-making and cheese-making, are now tourist attractions. Its fascinating museum (housed in the former station) is based on a comprehensive collection of artefacts which illustrate how people lived and worked in the dales in previous generations and how this influenced the development of the landscape. The museum complex incorporates the town's tourist information centre.

The Dales Countryside Museum is located in the Station Yard, off the A684 on the Leyburn side of Hawes.
Open April–October inclusive, 10–5. Telephone: (01969) 667450.

Hawes Ropemakers (W. R. Outhwaite & Son). Watch the thin strands of yarn being rapidly twisted into a strong rope in the traditional way. Admission free. Shop. Situated by the car park on the A684, opposite the children's playground.
Open Mondays–Fridays all year (except Christmas) 9–5.30, Bank Holiday Mondays and some Saturdays in summer.

Wensleydale Creamery. Visitors can see real Wensleydale cheese being made by hand, an industry started in Hawes in 1897, and enjoy 'The Cheese Experience', an organised tour. There is also a museum, shop and restaurant. The creamery is situated on Gayle Lane on the southern side of the town.
Open throughout the year, Mondays–Saturdays 9.30–5. Sundays 10–4.30. There are facilities for the disabled. Telephone: (01969) 667664.

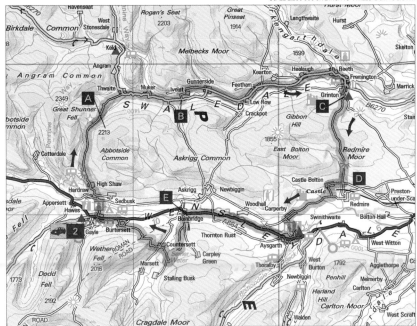

hotel at Simonstone and ascends a 1-in-6 gradient to the open moor. There is a fine view from just beyond the cattle-grid. The road skirts the flank of a hill appropriately called Lovely Seat, on the right. There is a parking place at the summit of the pass, at 1,726 feet (526 m), and others a little further on for those who wish to visit the Butter Tubs **A** from which the pass takes its name.

The Butter Tubs are precipitous shafts up to 78 feet (24 m) deep which were made by the action of rainwater on limestone. They may have taken their name from local farmers using them as a primitive cold store for their butter. Take care in examining them as the rock is very slippery when wet.

Continue the route descending steeply down to the village of Thwaite. Care is needed here as the road twists and there are gradients of 1-in-4 with a sheer drop to the right, so do not be too distracted by the magnificent views over Swaledale!

When you reach the B6270 turn right away from Thwaite heading towards Muker.

This is a busy little road, quite narrow with numerous bends. Muker has a small church with a distinctive white clock-face in its tower. It also has a pub, tearoom and shop.

Continue along the twisty road and ignore a turning to Askrigg on the right. Keep on the B6270 and, about 1 mile past the road to Askrigg, turn left B. This is a concealed turning which comes upon you suddenly, immediately after a small bridge. This lane leads to one of the most enchanting features of the Dales – the tiny humpbacked bridge at Ivelet. There are lovely picnic places by the riverside, before and after the bridge. The lane passes a telephone-box and then twists steeply up to reach a cattle-grid. There is a breathtaking vista from here of Swaledale.

At the top of the hill the lane forks – bear right and descend to a bridge and another cattle-grid. The lane

Hardraw Force

Semer Water at dusk

now runs eastwards high on the side of the valley, dropping steadily down to Gunnerside. **Rejoin the B6270 opposite the King's Head and continue straight on towards Reeth.**

This road soon meets up with the river close to the right. There are more lovely views over the hamlet of Crackpot as the road climbs some way above the river. Note that, although narrow, this is still a busy road with few passing places.

Continue on the B6270 passing through a hamlet called Low Row and then another called Feetham. On the outskirts of Reeth the road winds through a hamlet of stone cottages and old farm buildings.

The road dips down into Reeth, a town grouped around a large green. Turn right here, following the sign to Leyburn, and descend to the bottom of the valley to cross the Arkle Beck and

reach Fremington. **Go through the village keeping on the B6270. Cross the bridge over the River Swale into Grinton. At the Bridge Inn go straight on following the sign to Redmire and Leyburn, leaving the main road which bends to the left.** The road climbs steadily to reach the moor. **Cross the cattle-grid and then turn right at a road junction following the sign to Redmire C.**

Pause at some point during the long climb that follows and look back over Swaledale. If the conditions are right, the view will seem to extend to infinity. After the summit the view opens up ahead over Wensleydale and the fells beyond. Note the viewpoint marked on the map just above the old quarries which are to the left of the road.

The final stretch down to Redmire descends a gradient of 1-in-7. It is easy to miss the lane on the right D signposted to Castle Bolton. Heavy vehicles are banned from this road. The road twists down to a bridge and, as it climbs again into the village, the ruins of the castle may be seen ahead. The little church here is dwarfed by the crumbling towers of the castle which has been hailed as the climax of English military architecture.

After the castle the road descends steeply and crosses a disused railway to reach a main road. Turn right towards Aysgarth Falls and continue to the village of Carperby. Carperby was granted a market charter in 1305 and there is a stone market cross at its centre. **Turn left at the end of the village still heading for Aysgarth Falls.** The road drops down steeply, passing the National Park centre and car park on the right just after another old railway bridge crosses the road. The footpaths to the waterfalls are on the left side of the road, but to visit them you must park at the official

---

• PLACES OF INTEREST •

Bolton Castle
The castle was built by Richard le Scrope, Lord Chancellor of England in the reign of King Richard II. Work began in 1378,

and there is a local tradition that ox blood was mixed into the mortar to give extra strength. It took eighteen years to complete, and its medieval architect designed it with comfort and convenience in mind as much as defence. There were four huge, five-storey towers at the corners, with a magnificent gatehouse on the eastern side. Between the towers there were ranges of domestic quarters – stables,

brewhouse, laundry etc.

Mary Queen of Scots was a prisoner here for six months in 1568, and in 1645 the castle was besieged by Cromwell's army. It eventually surrendered and was then 'slighted' (made undefendable). This process so weakened the fabric that one of the towers collapsed during a storm in 1761. However, apart from this the walls still rise to their original height, and the impression as one approaches the remains, is one of menacing power. After the eighteenth century the great building was left as a romantic ruin, though parts have now been restored so that visitors can see tableaux of life as it was in the castle's heyday. The dungeons and battlements can also be explored – the latter giving wonderful views over the surrounding countryside.

Open March–November 10–5. Refreshments and shop. Telephone: (01969) 23981.

car park.

Continue down to cross Yore Bridge over the River Ure. There is a mill here housing a carriage and fire engine museum. **Climb steeply to the main road and turn right on to the A684 and pass through Aysgarth village**.

The main road follows the southern bank of the river through Worton. If you look across the river just before the village you will see an ancient house on the northern side of the valley. This is Nappa Hall where Mary Queen of Scots was once kept prisoner and where her ghost is still supposed to walk.

As you approach Bainbridge look for a lane on the left E which goes to Semer Water and Stalling Busk. At Bainbridge, as at Ripon, there is an official horn-blower who gives three blasts on the horn to each point of the compass. This custom takes place every night from 28 September until Shrove Tuesday, and was originally meant as a homing call to the shepherds on the hillsides around the village. The horn-blowers usually belong to the Metcalfe family whose

Hawes – a delightful market town in Wensleydale

ancestral home is Nappa Hall.

There are remains of a Roman fort, opposite the turning to Semer Water, showing that Wensleydale was strategically important to the Romans. **This lane follows the course of the River Bain and, when the road divides bear right. Two miles further on, at a T-junction, turn sharply to the right to reach Semer Water.** This is one of the scenic gems of the Yorkshire Dales. There is shoreside parking here, and a choice of footpaths to explore leading up into Raydale. A drowned village is supposed to lie beneath the waters, inundated because its inhabitants, who were

renowned for their selfishness, refused to shelter either an angel or a witch (depending on what version you hear).

Beyond the lake the road climbs steeply. Turn right and then left at Countersett, on the road which continues to climb a hill called Green Scar. At the top, where you cross a Roman road which led from Bainbridge to Ingleton, there are wonderful views looking back. **The modern road descends into the hamlet of Burtersett. Follow it through the village to pass a telephone-box and reach the A684 where you turn left to return to Hawes.** ■

Raydale seen from above Countersett

HAWES AND KETTLEWELL VIA COVERDALE

50 MILES – 2½ HOURS
START AND FINISH AT HAWES

This tour, which could be entitled 'Herriot Country' since it covers the area portrayed in the famous vet's novels, follows the northern side of Wensleydale at first before crossing to the opposite side at Aysgarth. A little further on it leaves Wensleydale to reach Coverdale, a lovely dale often neglected by visitors. After this the way crosses the watershed and descends into Wharfedale down the notorious Park Rash which has gradients of 1-in-4. The latter part of the tour begins at Kettlewell and follows Wharfedale and Langstrothdale up to the boggy wilderness of Dodd Fell. From here the road drops down Sleddale to return to the more hospitable scenery of Wensleydale.

From the Dales Countryside Museum car park at Hawes turn right round the traffic island to cross the one-way system, taking the road northwards towards Muker. Cross the elegant bridge over the River Ure and then turn right at the T-junction towards Askrigg and Sedbusk.

The road follows the northern side of Wensleydale, and in medieval times this was the main route along the valley. There are fine views to the right over Hawes and the surrounding hills. **Keep on this road through Askrigg.** This village was made famous by the television series *All Creatures Great and Small* in which Cringley House, facing the market cross, was renamed 'Skeldale House'.

Climb the hill past terraces of stone cottages and bear right on to the road signposted to Leyburn and Carperby. The hill out of the village is quite steep. About 1½ miles from Askrigg there is a group of houses on the left at Nappa Scar A. If you leave the car here for a moment you can walk a few yards further along the road and then take a driveway to the right which is part of a footpath leading down to the river. There is a good view of Nappa Hall from here.

Continue along the road as it passes by the hamlet of Woodhall. The steep escarpment

---

• PLACES OF INTEREST •

Wensleydale
Wensleydale is the most famous of the Yorkshire Dales, only rivalled by Wharfedale. It would be logical to think that it would be named Uredale, after the river which runs through it. Instead, it takes its name from the tiny village of Wensley, just beyond West Witton, on the A684. Until 1563 Wensley was the foremost market town in the Ure valley. However, in that year the village was virtually wiped out by plague and was never able to regain its importance over Hawes and Leyburn. Wensley church is worth seeing for the ornate private pew of the dukes of Bolton which resembles a box in an opera house.

Nappa Hall
This is a beautiful fifteenth-century fortified farmhouse built by Thomas Metcalfe, steward of the abbot of Jervaulx and warden of the Royal Forest of Wensleydale. The Metcalfes were said to be the largest family in England in the sixteenth century, and were certainly one of the most powerful in these parts. In 1556 three hundred Metcalfes, all mounted on white horses, attended Sir Christopher Metcalfe, High Sheriff of Yorkshire, at the York assizes. Nappa Hall served as a prison for Mary Queen of Scots for eighteen months from 1567, and her ghost is still supposed to walk there – you can check this out since the hall is a guest-house.

is on the left scarred by old mine workings. **Just after the village sign of Carperby, turn right following a sign to Aysgarth Falls. Go beneath an old railway bridge and past the National Park car park on the right. When the road meets with the A684 at Aysgarth, turn left towards Leyburn. The road passes beneath a pleasant canopy of trees into the hamlet of Swinithwaite and then comes to West Witton.** The village is celebrated for its bonfire ceremony which takes place in August, on the Saturday following St Bartholomew's Day. The effigy of this saint, 'Owd Bartle', is paraded and then burnt. The origins of the practice are probably pagan. The tower which stands on a hillside just to the east of West Witton was built by the third Duke of Bolton in remembrance of his actress wife, Lavinia Fenton, who initiated the role of Polly Peachum in *The Beggars' Opera*.

The Upper Falls at Aysgarth

Approximately 100 yards (91 m) after the Fox and Hounds Inn take the concealed turn to the right 🅱 **to Melmerby and Carlton.** The road climbs steeply and there are difficult hairpin bends to negotiate. Spectacular views open up to the left and to the rear, and it is worth stopping to enjoy these.

When the road divides at the top take the left fork to Middleham. Plenty of picnic places can be found along this beautiful part of the route. There are horse gallops to the right. **At a T-junction turn right towards Carlton and Kettlewell descending quite steeply into Agglethorpe. Just as you come to the first buildings of the village look for a concealed turn on the left signposted to Coverham and Middleham. This narrow, tree-shaded lane twists down to another T-junction. Turn left here.** After about 1 mile you will come to Coverham church

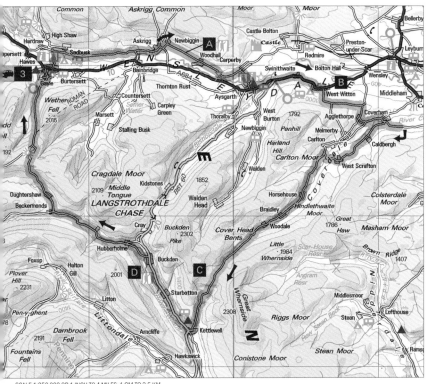

SCALE 1:250 000 OR 1 INCH TO 4 MILES *1 CM TO 2.5 KM*

The River Ure at Hawes

and the bridge over the lovely River Cover. This spot is haunted by a Black Lady who walks from the churchyard. The skeleton of a woman was found nearby in the 1940s – she was wearing a decayed black dress.

Turn right before the church to cross the bridge and head for Caldbergh and West Scrafton. (If you wish to visit Braithwaite Hall turn left just after the bridge.) This narrow byway, with very few passing places, takes you through a delightful, unfrequented dale.

The road goes through a series of small hamlets, the largest being West Scrafton, and then crosses over the River Cover again to reach a major road at a T-junction. Turn left towards Kettlewell. This is a wider lane, which passes by a succession of isolated farms and cottages. The hamlet of Horsehouse is the place where horses were changed when this was a busy pack-horse route. The small community of Arkleside makes a picturesque sight – a scattering of farms clinging to the hillside on the far side of the river. The road is soon up on the open moor and you can see it for miles ahead snaking over the barren countryside. **At Coverhead Farm it descends down a 1-in-7 gradient to cross the river over a stone bridge.** Here there are many places where you can have a picnic. **About 2 miles on from the bridge you pass a stone pillar C called the Hunter's Stone.** There is a grand view back from here.

From this point the road begins its descent to Wharfedale, at times down steep gradients with hairpin bends. The overhanging Kilnsey Crag beyond Kettlewell can be seen from here. **There is a final 1-in-5 descent into the village itself. Turn right opposite the post office and then immediately left. When you**

• PLACES OF INTEREST •

Aysgarth Falls
It is best to park at the car park by the National Park Information Centre if you wish to take in the full splendour of the waterfalls. You will catch a glimpse of the Upper Falls as you cross the bridge into the village. The Lower Falls have a much more romantic setting, and are only reached by way of the footpaths which leave from the road, before and after the bridge. Altogether the falls cover nearly 1 mile of the wooded course of the River Ure as it descends over a series of rock ledges.

Yore Mill, by the bridge, was built in 1784 as a worsted mill, later converted to spin cotton, was burnt down, and then became a grain mill. It now houses the Yorkshire Museum of Carriages and Horse Drawn Vehicles.

Yore Mill. Open Good Friday until October, daily 11–5. Telephone: (01748) 823275.

Wensleydale Creamery, Hawes
Visitors can see real Wensleydale cheese being made by hand, an industry started in Hawes in 1897, and enjoy 'The Cheese Experience', an organised tour. There is also a museum, shop and restaurant. The creamery is situated on Gayle Lane on the southern side of the town.

Open throughout the year, Mondays– Saturdays 9.30–5. Sundays 10–4.30. There are facilities for the disabled. Telephone: (01969) 667664.

Langstrothdale
Wharfedale becomes Langstrothdale above Buckden. This was once a hunting forest belonging to the Percy family who maintained ten lodges in the dale. Thus, the name Buckden refers to the quarry of the noble huntsmen.

Before the coming of the Percys, Bronze Age people lived here, and there are remains of a stone circle at Yockenthwaite. In the Dark Ages, Viking invaders settled in the valley, clearing the ground to allow grazing for their sheep.

When the Percys acquired the land they cleared out most of the existing settlement, and those that continued to live there had to abide with a harsh system of forest law. Poaching was a capital offence.

Braithwaite Hall
This National Trust property is a large mid-seventeenth-century house. It has some excellent panelling and furnishings.

You will be able to see the building from the road, but appointments have to be made with the tenant should you wish to visit. Telephone: Mrs D. Duffus (01969) 40287.

reach the main road, turn right on to the B6160, heading up Wharfedale with the river to the left. The scenery is typical of Upper Wharfedale with the valley flat and wide with steep, wooded sides.

The next village is Starbotton which is followed by Buckden. Turn left here **D** to Hubberholme and Hawes. The church, dedicated to St Michael and All Angels, stands by the bridge at Hubberholme. It dates from Norman times and is notable for its sixteenth-century rood-loft. Its pews are the work of the 'Mouseman', Robert Thompson of Kilburn, who delighted in hiding carvings of mice in his work – see if you can find them here. J. B. Priestley, one of Yorkshire's best-loved writers, requested that his ashes should be scattered in this peaceful churchyard.

Keep to the main road which, swooping and dipping, soon reaches open moorland again as it climbs up Langstrothdale and passes through the village of Deepdale. This is a very popular road with picnickers as the river is close by.

The lovely church at Hubberholme

The road steadily climbs to the top of Dodd Fell where there is a car park and viewpoint. At this point you enter Richmondshire and are on the highest road in North Yorkshire at 1,934 feet (589 m). There is a magnificent view ahead as the road begins a 1-in-4 descent down Park Rash.

A blind summit follows this, so do not relax when the steep descent ends. There are views of Hawes in its moorland setting as the road drops down to the township of Gayle. **You will pass the Wensleydale Creamery before coming to Hawes.** ∎

Langstrothdale in typical dale's weather

SWALEDALE AND ARKENGARTHDALE

52 MILES – 2¹/₂ HOURS
START AND FINISH AT RICHMOND

This figure-of-eight route takes the traveller through a fascinating medley of scenery. First, there is the rich woodland and pastures which line Swaledale upstream from Richmond. Then, from Reeth, it strikes north-westwards to follow Arkengarthdale, the landscape growing wilder mile by mile. The return begins from the summit of Tan Hill and crosses the bleakly beautiful Stonesdale Moor to drop down into Swaledale again, following the dale back to Richmond. The final leg uses the road on the north side of the valley which gives a different aspect to its scenery.

• PLACES OF INTEREST •

Richmond
This is the capital of Swaledale, a town dominated by the massive keep of its castle which looks down on the red pantiles of the houses surrounding it. Many of these date from Georgian times and line the very steep streets which give Richmond its rare and beautiful character.

The castle was erected by one of William I's most trusted supporters, Alan the Red of Brittany, who died in 1089. However, the 100-foot- (30.5 m) high central keep dates from the following century, and its construction reflects the strategic importance of Richmond. At this time North Yorkshire was still being harried by raiding parties from Scotland. It is appropriate that such a symbol of military might stands here, since Richmond has been a garrison town for generations, Catterick Camp being but 4 miles away. Furthermore, the Regimental Museum of the Green Howards occupies the former Trinity Church overlooking the market-place.

The Georgian theatre stands in contrast to the town's martial character. Patrons can enjoy plays and concerts in a magnificent setting which exactly matches the original. If you are unable to see a production, there are daytime guided tours round the theatre and its museum, which has a collection of old playbills and a complete set of painted scenery dating from 1836.

Richmond Castle (English Heritage) is open April–September daily 10–6. October–March Wednesdays– Sundays 10–4. Telephone: (01748) 822493.

Green Howards Museum, Trinity Church Square. Open February Mondays–Fridays 9.15–4.30. March and November Mondays–Saturdays 9.15–4.30. April–October Mondays–Saturdays 9.15–4.30. Sundays 2–4.30.

Richmond Theatre Royal Museum, Victoria Road. Open Easter Saturday–31 October. Mondays–Saturdays 11–4.45 Sundays 2.30–4.45. Telephone: (01748) 823021.

From Richmond take the A6108 westwards out of town towards Reeth and Leyburn. The road follows the north bank of the River Swale initially, but then crosses to the south bank approximately 1 mile beyond the picnic place and caravan site at Roundham.

There are soon fine views up Swaledale with its wooded slopes. **Keep ahead on the B6270 to Reeth when the Leyburn road bends to the left.** A little further on you can see Marrick Priory on the northern bank of the river. However, there are other monastic remains closer at hand, at Ellerton near to the road on the southern side. Cistercian nuns occupied Ellerton whilst their neighbours at Marrick were Benedictines.

The road twists down into the village of Grinton. Follow the B6270 across the bridge and into Fremington. Cross another bridge, this time over the Arkle Beck, into Reeth. Climb up to the spacious green and then fork right to Arkengarthdale A by the Buck Hotel. The road quickly climbs to open moorland.

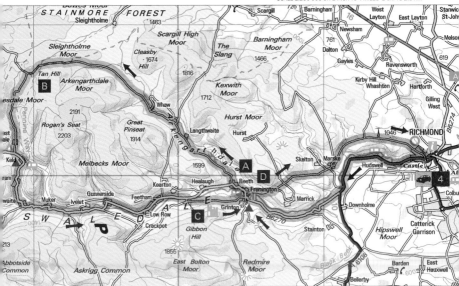

Arkengarthdale is a splendid dale, its small farms hugging the sides of the valley connected to each other by a filigree of stone walls. Arkengarthdale's sheep seem to be unaware of traffic, or perhaps simply enjoy bringing cars to an abrupt halt! The road can be seen in the distance twisting up the dale.

There is a steep descent into Langthwaite. This is a village which owes its origin to the lead mines which brought a degree of prosperity to the dale in the nineteenth century. Langthwaite has a church between two pubs, and there is a place appropriately named Booze at the end of the cul-de-sac leading up the daleside from the Red Lion. The name Booze derives from a Norse word meaning 'the house by the curve in the way'. An alternative theory is that it is a contraction of 'bull-house'.

Keep straight on at the junction where a road leaves to the right to Barnard Castle. The road climbs steadily and the landscape becomes gradually more bleak. There is another curiously-named settlement to the right – Whaw – and this is the last place of any size in the dale apart from isolated farms. As the road continues to climb

the views become ever more extensive, stretching to the hills of Northumbria. The naturalist will enjoy seeing many pairs of curlew, but may not appreciate seeing the innumerable shooting butts which are also a feature of the landscape.

Eventually, the road reaches Tan Hill, England's highest pub.

There are magnificent views from here over the three counties which meet at this lonely point – Yorkshire, Cumbria and Durham. It is easy to see traffic moving on the A66, 5 miles or so to the north. The view to the west is also superb, one good reason for making a morning start on this route.

The castle overlooking Richmond

27

Just after the pub turn left **B** to Thwaite (22 miles). As the road descends into West Stones Dale isolated farms appear on the hillsides. The descent steepens before the tiny hamlet of West Stonesdale which consists of two farms and a telephone-box. **The final way down into Swaledale is very pretty, but care is needed since the gradient is 1-in-4 at one**

A laithe (field barn) near Keld

stage. When you meet the B6270 turn left into Keld. This point marks the beginning of Swaledale proper, where the bleak moors to the west give way to pastures enclosed by stone walls. The main part of the village is to the left of the main road, and there is a pleasant walk from the church to Kisdon Force, a cataract just to the east of the village.

Follow the B6270

southwards through Thwaite and then Muker. These two villages were founded by Norse settlers. The church at Muker dates from 1580, and before that Grinton had to serve the needs of Upper Swaledale. Thus, the dead were carried for long distances from remote farms, and a Corpse Way was established for these processions. Bodies were carried in wicker baskets, and there were special stones where the baskets were put down when the bearers rested. One of these stones is to be found about 2 miles east of Muker, by the first gateway in the lane leading down to Ivelet Bridge.

Keep on the main road from Muker to Gunnerside where the road bends left to cross the River Swale. Pass through the village of Low Row and, about 1 1/2 miles further on, turn right to cross the river following a sign to Askrigg. Turn left after the bridge C on to a quiet byway signposted to Grinton. This lane climbs high on the side of the dale to give magnificent views over Reeth to the high moorland beyond, the river meandering in the foreground. To the right you

Reeth

It is hard to imagine this beautiful town, set around a spacious triangular green, as a bustling mining town, but in its heyday it must have resembled Klondike. The surrounding hills were riddled with lead mines, and the industry was controlled from Reeth until, in the decade after 1875, it went into sudden decline leaving five thousand miners without jobs and the mines and smelt mills derelict. The town was fortunate in having other interests to save it from extinction. Its setting is splendid, and the decline in mining took place just as tourists were beginning to discover the dales. Its lack of a railway gave it a sort of exclusivity in the 1920s and 1930s when it was a very popular venue for charabanc outings. Furthermore, Reeth was a flourishing market centre for Swaledale and Arkengarthdale (it has a market charter signed in 1695) and it also had a hand-knitting industry (though this too was in decline). Visitors curious to find out more should visit the folk museum on the green.

The Swaledale Folk Museum, Reeth Green. The museum reflects the history, traditions and social history of the district with exhibits illustrating lead mining, knitting, domestic and religious artefacts, etc.

Open Good Friday–31 October daily 10.30–5.30. Telephone: (01748) 84373.

Tan Hill

At 1,732 feet (528 m), Tan Hill is England's highest pub. It lies on the Pennine Way, and thus fulfills a useful function in refreshing weary walkers, though it was originally built in the eighteenth century to serve drovers and coal miners.

Coal was mined at Tan Hill in medieval times and the colliery was finally closed in the 1930s. In May a large sheep fair is held on Tan Hill, and attracts farmers from all over northern England and even Scotland. Swaledale sheep are exceptionally hardy and are always in demand by shepherds keen to improve their stock.

will see the 16-foot- (4.9 m) high ramparts of Maiden Castle, an Iron Age hill-fort. There are fine sites for picnics here.

The lane descends to Grinton, coming out by the church. This is often called the 'Cathedral of the Dales'. **Turn left and keep straight on to cross the bridge. Take the first turning right after this, signposted to Marrick and Marske** **.** The lane is twisting and narrow and some care is needed. To the right there is a lane going to Marrick Priory, which now serves as an outdoor educational training centre. The remains of the twelfth-century Benedictine priory are private, though they may be viewed from the grounds. Beyond this turning the road is steep, but gives wonderful views down Swaledale. Parking is available in laybys so that this view may be enjoyed.

Pass the turning to Marrick village, then go straight over the crossroads which follows. Descend a 1-in-6 gradient into Marske. Keep straight on to stay on the road to Whashton and Ravensworth when the road to Richmond and Leyburn leads off to the

right. There are lovely views of Swaledale as the road climbs steadily. **About 3 miles from Marske a road leaves to the left to Whashton – keep ahead here and pass a wireless mast.** The monument on a crag to the right of the road opposite the mast was erected by Robert Willance in 1606 after he became lost in fog and fell from the escarpment. Willance broke his leg in the fall and his horse

was killed. However, he had the presence of mind to slit open the dead animal and insert his damaged limb into its belly, thus keeping it warm and saving his life. **From here there is a steady descent into Richmond.** Its castle can be seen from time to time through or above the foliage. **At the T-junction you will meet the A6108, the road from which the tour began.** ■

Muker in Swaledale

29

..ON, MASHAM, ..IDDERDALE AND FOUNTAINS ABBEY

50 MILES – 2½ HOURS
START AND FINISH AT RIPON

There is something to please all tastes in this tour. At first the route follows the course of the River Ure to Masham. It then strikes south-westwards across increasingly wild country to reach Nidderdale, the most unjustly neglected of the dales. After following this dale to Pateley Bridge, the route passes Brimham Rocks to reach a trio of National Trust properties – Fountains Hall, Fountains Abbey and Studley Royal – before returning to Ripon.

Take the A61 (Thirsk road) out of Ripon, crossing the River Ure and climbing the hill up the side of the valley. Be very careful not to miss the turning to the left A, which leaves before the top of the hill is reached, and goes to Hutton Conyers. However, if you miss this turn there is another about 1 mile further on, which leads to the same village.

After approximately 3 miles you will come to Norton Conyers House. The gardens are open to the public at most times, though the house less frequently. The building is late-medieval, though substantial additions were made in Stuart and Georgian times. The pictures, furniture, china and costumes reflect the years of ownership by the same family.

Continue on the road past the house but, just before you get to the village of Wath, turn left to Tanfield. The road goes close to the river just before West Tanfield, where you join with the A6108 to Masham and Leyburn. The church and Marmion Tower are to the left – the latter is the gatehouse of a castle built by the Marmion family, celebrated in one of the works of Sir Walter Scott. The rest of the castle has disappeared. Effigies of several members of the family may be seen on chest-tombs in the church.

Continue along the A6108 to Masham where the road swings west to cross the river and reach the town centre. Masham has a grand church. Its vast market-place is a reminder that it was of considerable importance in medieval times, with a charter granting it a market and two annual fairs. One of the fairs lives on in the form of the annual sheep sales. This takes place early in autumn and brings

Fountains Abbey, the climax of this tour

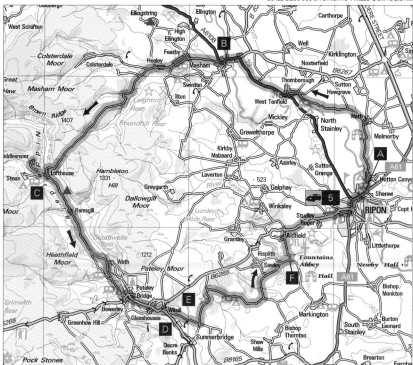

buyers from afar, many seeking the sheep which take their name from the town – cross-bred ewes with a uniquely crinkly fleece. There are also two breweries here, one of which, Theakston's, has a visitors' centre

On the outskirts of the town turn left B, off the A6108, on to a road signposted to Leighton Reservoir. Continue through Fearby with its wide village green. Fearby almost seems joined to the next village of Healey. The road descends a steep hill to cross the River Burn and then climbs even more steeply on the other side to reach Leighton. Leighton Dam is $1/2$ mile on from the village, and the road skirts the western shore of the reservoir. There is another steep climb away from the reservoir and the road soon reaches open moorland.

After about 3 miles of open moorland the road crosses a cattle-grid and begins its descent into Nidderdale. It is difficult to concentrate on the

• *PLACES OF INTEREST* •

Ripon
The minster was granted cathedral status in 1836, and so Ripon became a city. Although small, it is crammed with interest. The cathedral stands on the site of an abbey founded by Bishop Wilfred in 664. The undercroft of Wilfred's Church is beneath

the massive central tower of the cathedral and is shown to visitors. It is the oldest crypt in Europe outside Italy. Other glories of the cathedral are the exquisitely-carved fifteenth-century choir stalls and misericords and the magnificent Early English west front.

Daniel Defoe thought Ripon's market-place to be the finest in England and, in spite of being used as a car park for much of the time, it still manages to retain its splendour, thanks to the buildings which surround it. One of these, on the south side, is the sixteenth-century Wakeman's House, easily recognised as it is the only half-timbered building in the vicinity. The Wakeman's duties originated in Saxon times (he was overseer of the night-watchmen) and one of these is maintained to this day. At nine o'clock every evening he arrives in ornate dress to blow his horn at each corner of the square, in theory so that the watchmen may be inspected.

Ripon Prison and Police Museum, St Marygate. This uses fascinating memorabilia to depict the story of our police and shows how criminals in Victorian times served their sentences.

Open April–October weekdays 1–5. (except July and August 11–5). All Sundays 1–5. Telephone: (01765) 603006.

steep and winding road when the view ahead is so spectacular. Middlesmoor church is a dominant feature, situated on the side of the hill ahead overlooking the extent of Nidderdale.

The road comes to a T-junction at Lofthouse C**. Turn right here to drive up to Middlesmoor.** There is a car park here. How Stean Gorge, with its famous caves, is reached by way of a lane off to the left of the road to Middlesmoor.

Return to Lofthouse and keep on through the village to reach Ramsgill at the top of the Gouthwaite Reservoir. The road follows the shore of the reservoir. There is a picnic place to the right and a bird-watcher's observation post close to the reservoir, about halfway along. Like the Scar House Reservoir above it, Gouthwaite supplies Bradford with water – it was built between 1893 and 1901. **Continue straight on past the**

Gouthwaite Reservoir

Watermill Inn. This was a yarn spinning-mill until 1966 – its giant 35-foot (10.7 m) water-wheel may still be seen.

At Pateley Bridge turn left on to the B6265 and cross the bridge into the town. There are many places to stop for refreshment and, at the right time

of year, it is adorned with brightly-coloured hanging baskets.

Continue on the main road eastwards out of Pateley Bridge and keep straight on when the B6265 (Ripon road) goes off to the left. You are now on the B6165 Ripley and Summerbridge road, and will soon pass through a village called Glasshouses. Pass the Birch Tree Inn to enter the next village, Wilsill. Take the second turning to the left D **along a lane to Smelthouses.** This place obviously took its name from the lead industry which once flourished here. The lane dips down a 1-in-7 gradient and then climbs sharply through woods. **At a crossroads which follows turn left to Brimham Rocks.**

The weirdly-eroded gritstone rocks E are a National Trust property and are remarkably similar to the tors of Dartmoor – so much so that a version of *Hound of the Baskervilles* was filmed here. Most of them have nicknames like 'The Dancing Bear' or 'The Druid's Writing Desk' – ancient folklore had it that the rocks were sculpted by Druids. Children love the scrambles they provide, though care is needed as some of the rocks are 30 feet (9 m) or more high. Grown-ups will enjoy the views over Nidderdale. The official National Trust car park is on the left of the road, but there are plenty of other parking and picnic places on the right-hand side of the road which allow access to the rocks.

Turn right at the next road junction following the sign to Warsill and Bishop Thornton. Keep on the main road past a turning to Warsill on the right. There are lovely landscapes to enjoy here as the road winds its way around Rabbit Hill. Note the tower on the hill ahead as you approach the next T-junction – it is a sham ruin built in the eighteenth century and was the first landscape feature of the

Pateley Bridge

The Moon Pond and Temple of Piety, Studley Royal

Studley Park water garden. **Turn left at the T-junction to Sawley and Grantley.** The road descends very steeply before climbing again past Sawley Hall. **Ignore a turn on the left here which goes to Sawley village and keep on towards Fountains Abbey.** The abbey is only revealed at the last moment as you come down the hill to the bridge across the River Skell ▢. After the bridge the road bends round the perimeter of the abbey – the car park for Fountains Abbey and Studley Park is reached by a road off to the right. **If you do not wish to visit either of these properties keep straight on to reach the B6265 and turn right to pass another entrance to** **Fountains Abbey.** A little further on is a turning on the right to Studley Roger – many people prefer to reach the abbey from this side, although it entails a mile-long walk through the water gardens. The wonderful view of the abbey comes as a climax when it is revealed. **The outskirts of Ripon are only a short distance from this point.** ▪

• PLACES OF INTEREST •

How Stean Gorge
Thousands of years ago a tiny beck found a narrow stratum of limestone sandwiched between hard gritstone and etched its way remorselessly through to make a miniature, but very picturesque, gorge often called 'Yorkshire's Little Switzerland'.

Children enjoy visiting Tom Taylor's Cave from the gorge, and torches are provided at the shop to help in the exploration of the 530-foot- (162 m) long passageway. It is named after a highwayman who used it as a hideout.

Nidderdale Museum
Situated in the Council Offices, Pateley Bridge. Here there are reconstructions of cobbler's, chemist's, and haberdasher's shops as they looked in the past. It has a wide variety of other exhibits illustrating life in the district in the past. Telephone: (01423) 711225.

Fountains Abbey and Studley Royal
A group of Cistercian monks from York came here in 1132 to set up an alternative community dedicated to St Mary of the Fountains because they believed that their life in York was too undemanding. At that time the wooded site they chose was considered to be more suited for wild beasts than Men of God, yet the abbey they founded became one of the richest in England, controlling one million acres and supporting six hundred lay brothers as well as monks. The ruins reflect this prosperity and are of striking beauty, set in a park landscaped to make them the centre-piece.

The adjoining Studley Royal (which shares with Fountains Abbey the distinction of being a World Heritage site) has the best surviving Georgian Green Water Garden with lakes, temples and cascades presenting a succession of breath-taking vistas. Studley Hall was burnt down in 1946, but fortunately the magnificent garden survives, and the price of admission includes two more buildings – the remarkable Church of St Mary's built by William Burges 1871 to 1878, and the Jacobean Fountains Hall which houses an exhibition on the abbey.

Fountains Abbey and Studley Royal Water Garden are open all the year daily except on Fridays in November, December and January (and at Christmas). From April–September 10–7, October–March 10–5 (or dusk if earlier). Shop, restaurant and tearoom. Telephone: (01765) 608888 or 601005.

HELMSLEY, BYLAND ABBEY AND THE HAMBLETON HILLS

46 MILES - 2 HOURS
START AND FINISH AT HELMSLEY

This tour takes you through the flat lands of the Vale of Pickering to see Nunnington House and Hovingham village before turning westwards towards the Hambleton Hills. You will pass through more delightful villages and see Byland Abbey before climbing to the top of Sutton Bank, a wonderful viewpoint. The route then follows the crest of the ridge for a time before turning eastwards. The finale is a visit to Rievaulx Abbey, a memorable climax to a tour which blends history with beautiful scenery.

Leave Helmsley on the A170 towards Scarborough. Pass through Beadlam and Nawton. These villages are now joined along the main road and share the church at Beadlam. **After the road has made a sweeping right-hand turn, take the road to the right A, following a sign to Wombleton and Nunnington.** The former has the wide main street usual in the Vale of Pickering. Its pub, the Plough, is built using the cruck form of construction which was probably introduced by the Danes.

At the end of the village branch left towards Nunnington to pass Linton airfield to the right. This was a busy air base during the Second World War and the home of Fighter Command's first jet squadron. **Go straight over the crossroads which follows to cross over the River Rye into Nunnington.** The hall is to the left, and there is a good view of the house from the road. Nunnington Hall is in the care of the National Trust and dates from the sixteenth century, though substantial additions and alterations were made at the end of the following century. The attics contain the Carlisle Collection of miniature rooms, displaying the various styles of English domestic architecture.

• PLACES OF INTEREST •

Helmsley
This very pleasant old market town has come to depend on tourism for its livelihood, and this is reflected in the shops and hotels which face its square. Helmsley is a special delight in spring when daffodils cover the banks of the stream which flows by the street leading from the market place to the castle. This dates from 1186 and has a unique D-shaped keep, and an extensive Tudor domestic range where original plasterwork and panelling survive. Formidable defensive earthworks surround it. The castle stood here uneventfully for nearly five hundred years until suffering a three-month siege during the Civil War. After it surrendered the castle was made ruinous by General Fairfax's Roundheads. It is now cared for by English Heritage.
Helmsley Castle. Open daily April–September 10–6. October–March Wednesdays–Sundays 10–4. Telephone: (01439) 70442.

Duncombe Park
The family home of Lord and Lady Feversham is situated 1 mile south-west of Helmsley. It was originally built in the early eighteenth century for the Duncombe family (ancestors of the Fevershams) after Fairfax had left their previous home, Helmsley Castle, in ruins. It was probably designed by Vanbrugh, but was destroyed by fire in 1879. However, it was subsequently rebuilt to the original designs. The house has recently been renovated and is open to the public. The eighteenth-century landscaped garden (including a terrace with temples at each end) is surrounded by three hundred acres of parkland.
Duncombe Park is open at Easter 11–5. April and October on Wednesdays and Sundays 11–5 or dusk. May, June and September Sundays–Thursdays 11–5. July–August daily 11–5. Telephone: (01439) 70213.

Duncombe Park near Helmsley

East. Gilling Castle now serves as the preparatory school for Ampleforth College, but was once the seat of the Fairfax family. Although the castle has an eighteenth-century facade, parts of it date from earlier times – the Elizabethan Great Chamber has a wonderful ceiling and panelling which was purchased by Randolph Hearst and taken to America. Fortunately, the college was able to bring it back. Go straight through the village passing the drive to the castle (which is hidden by trees) to the left and the church to the right.

As you approach the next village of Oswaldkirk the red roofs of the buildings are prominent. **In Oswaldkirk the B1363 swings round to the right, but you turn left here C towards Ampleforth and Coxwold.** The lane passes Ampleforth College, a famous Catholic public school run by Benedictine monks. The abbey was founded by Benedictines who escaped from France during the Revolution and were given land here by the Fairfax family. You may care to visit the magnificent

Keep straight on towards Hovingham. The road descends Caulkleys Bank, and there is a lovely view southwards from the top. **Keep straight on to join the B1257 and enter Hovingham.** The Romans built a villa here, probably attracted by the spring which rises just to the west of the village. In the nineteenth century an attempt was made to use this spring as the basis for a spa which, it was hoped, would rival Harrogate. The Worsley family have occupied the splendid Palladian hall since the eighteenth century.

Turn right B opposite the Worsley Arms Hotel to Coulton, passing through the gates of Hovingham Park. This is a lovely part of the route, the lane winding through richly-timbered parkland and, at one stage, looking down on a delightful ornamental bridge. Beyond the park it climbs steadily to pass through Hovingham High Wood. **Turn right at the crossroads which follows towards Gilling. After about 2 miles this quiet lane joins the B1363 which takes you through the village of Gilling**

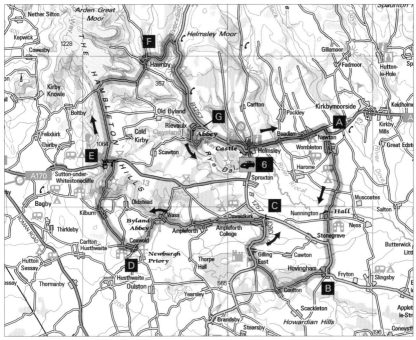

SCALE 1:250 000 OR 1 INCH TO 4 MILES *1 CM TO 2.5 KM*

35

abbey church, built to the designs of Sir Giles Gilbert Scott and only completed in 1961.

The road continues through the village of Ampleforth. Care should be taken on this road which is narrow and is frequented by caravans banned from using Sutton Bank. **The dramatic ruins of Byland Abbey are to the left as the road swings southwards towards Coxwold. Here there is a choice: turn left at the crossroads D if you wish to visit Newburgh Priory, less than 1 mile down the lane, or right to continue on the tour.** Pass the church with its unusual octagonal tower (inside there is a carving said to be by Grinling Gibbons) to come to a lovely old house on the right. This is Shandy Hall, the home of the eighteenth-century novelist Laurence Sterne who wrote *Tristram Shandy* and is buried in Coxwold churchyard. The hall is open to the public and contains many relics of the writer.

Three hundred yards (274 m) further on turn right towards Kilburn and then, almost immediately, bear left following the major road. There are excellent views of the famous White Horse as you approach the village. **Keep straight on through the village to climb White Horse Bank, bearing left when the main road continues to Oldstead.** You can park halfway up this hill in order to get close-up views of the horse, though it seems to be less life-like when viewed this way.

The road passes a glider field at the top of the bank and then goes through a forestry planting before meeting the A170. **Turn left and then take the first turning right E on to a road which strikes northwards along the top of the ridge towards Cold Kirby and Old Byland.** There is a car park here

• PLACES OF INTEREST •

Byland Abbey
Although much smaller than Rievaulx or Fountains, the abbey at Byland is full of interest, and is considered to be one of the dozen finest monastic ruins in Britain. It belonged to the Cistercian order and building began in 1177. The entire length of the north wall of the church can be seen. The west front is also well-preserved and must have had a magnificent rose window, 26 feet (7.9 m) in diameter – a feature more often seen in cathedrals. (English Heritage).

Open April–September daily 10–6. October–March Wednesdays–Saturdays 10–4. Telephone: (013476) 614.

Newburgh Priory
Little, if anything, survives of the fabric of the Augustinian monastery which occupied the site from 1145 until 1529. The present house has work of all periods from Tudor through to Georgian times, much of the building dating from 1732 (the year inscribed on the rainwater heads). The priory was the home of Cromwell's daughter, and his body, minus the head, is supposed to occupy a tomb within the house.

The gardens are notable for their topiary, the yew trees being cut into the shapes of birds and dogs, though the *pièce de résistance* is the coronet by the main drive.

House and grounds are open April–June Wednesdays and Sundays 2–6. Grounds only are open in July and August Wednesdays and Sundays 2–6. Telephone: (01347) 868435.

for those who wish to enjoy the magnificent view westwards from the top of Sutton Bank.

After about 1 mile bear left, when a road goes to the right to Cold Kirby. The road is now straight for nearly 4 miles. There are wide views to the right. **Turn right towards Hawnby when the road meets a T-junction** (the Boltby Forest Mountain Bike Trail continues straight ahead). Now there are views over a beautiful succession of landscapes, and a steep drop is suddenly revealed to the left above a farm called Dale Town. **After this the road drops steeply down a 1-in-4 gradient to Hawnby F and then climbs up into the village. Bear right here towards Osmotherley. At the next junction turn sharp right towards Laskill.** The initial section of this lane has a steep descent and ascent, but soon provides good views down into two valleys, those of the River Rye and then the River Seph.

When the road meets the B1257 turn right towards Helmsley. This road enters the Hambledon Forest with a picnic site on the left and a viewpoint to the right. **After about 4 miles take the turning to the right G to Rievaulx.** The entrance to Rievaulx Terrace is by this turn. There is a steep descent into

• PLACES OF INTEREST •

Kilburn
As you approach Kilburn the famous White Horse can be seen. It dates from 1857 and was the work of a local schoolmaster who, having seen the chalk figures of the South Downs, set his pupils the project of creating a similar design on the flank of Roulston Scar.

The Mouseman Visitor Centre is where Robert Thompson worked to produce exquisite carvings which may be seen at Ampleforth Abbey, York Minster and St Paul's Cathedral. He was known as the Mouseman through his delight in including a carving of a mouse in his work. His successors produce hand-crafted furniture from the workshop here.

Rievaulx Abbey
The ruins of the Cistercian monastery in the narrow, wooded valley are usually considered to be the most beautiful in Britain. The abbey was founded in 1132

and the choir, with its soaring arches, is one of the major glories of medieval architecture, dating from 1225. English Heritage have taken pains to explain the purpose of the various ancillary buildings which flanked the abbey church. The site was once occupied by a community of 140 monks and 600 lay people.

Open April–September daily 10–6. October–March 10–4. Telephone: (0143) 96228.

Rievaulx Terrace and Temples
Note that there is no access to the abbey from the terrace. The 1/2-mile grassy terrace (originally part of the Duncombe Park demesne) gives views over the abbey and over the Rye valley to the Hambleton Hills. There are two classical temples, the Ionic Temple having ceiling-paintings and an exhibition in its basement.

Open late March–end October 10.30–6 or dusk. No admission after 5. Telephone: (014396) 340.

the village with a good view of the abbey. The car park is on the left. The road follows a pretty stream where picnic places may be found.

Turn left at the road junction by the bridge towards Helmsley. If you

look to the left you will see another view of the abbey. **Turn right when this byway joins with the B1257 again.** The ruins of Helmsley Castle, with its startling white stone, can be seen ahead as you descend the hill into the town. ■

The Kilburn White Horse

HARROGATE, ILKLEY MOOR AND BOLTON ABBEY

58 MILES – 3 HOURS
START AND FINISH AT HARROGATE

This tour is full of interest, including famous beauty spots like Bolton Abbey and Ilkley Moor and lesser-known treasures such as Almscliff Crag and The Chevin – both magnificent viewpoints. The reservoirs in the Washburn valley, towards the end of the tour, provide convenient places to picnic, and garden-lovers will enjoy Harlow Car on the outskirts of Harrogate.

Cow and Calf Rocks, Ilkley

Leave Harrogate from The Stray on the B6162 to Beckwithshaw, heading westwards to pass the famous gardens at Harlow Car. These belong to the Northern Horticultural Society, and the sixty-eight acres include features which will interest all garden-lovers throughout the year. There is even a model village to please children. **Just before Beckwithshaw the road joins the B6161.** Pass the church and pub. **At the end of the village, where the main** road bends to the right, take the road on the left to Rigton. **Climb up the lane and continue straight over the crossroads to descend into North Rigton. At the Square and Compass pub turn right towards Huby and Otley to pass the church on the left. Then turn right again up Crag Lane towards Stainburn and Leathley.** This is a lovely road along the top of the ridge with wide views to the left. There are places to picnic. Almscliff Crag  is to the right, and is a favourite venue for rock-climbers as well as being a good viewpoint over lower Wharfedale. Those without ropes and pitons will find an easy way to the top via a path which climbs up the northern side.

• *PLACES OF INTEREST* •

Harrogate
The town has had a comparatively short, albeit chequered, history. In 1571 the first of its medicinal springs was discovered, and in 1598 a local man, Thomas Bright, paved a way to it. He called it a spa, deriving the name from the town in Belgium already famous for its health-giving waters. Strangely, the fashion for spas in the eighteenth century, which saw the growth of Bath and Cheltenham, did not touch Harrogate, and it was only in the following century that the place was able to promote its wells and springs and base its prosperity on them. Public baths were built, and eminent Victorians came to stay in the new hotels to take the waters and bathe in the sulphurous or iron-rich waters. However, the fashion for these 'cures' proved to be short-lived, and the town was in decline after the Second World War until people discovered the need for conferences and exhibitions. It is these gatherings which have rescued Harrogate's fortunes. For all that, the town is a very pleasant place to visit, with excellent shops and eating-places, while the far-sightedness of its early planners gave it the delightfully spacious commons on its southern side – The Stray, West Park, and Valley Gardens.

Ilkley
Like Harrogate, though on a smaller scale, Ilkley developed as a spa town in the nineteenth century. However, unlike its near neighbour, Ilkley had ancient origins. There was a Bronze Age settlement on the moor above, and the Romans maintained a strong garrison here to protect their road which ran from Manchester, through Ilkley, and then north-eastwards to Bainbridge in Wensleydale. The parish church stands on the site of the Roman fort. Ilkley was also important in medieval times for its market and rowdy annual fair. Its popularity as a spa town (it was known as 'the Malvern of the North') spanned the same years as Harrogate, and today it serves mainly as a pleasant dormitory for people working in Leeds and Bradford.

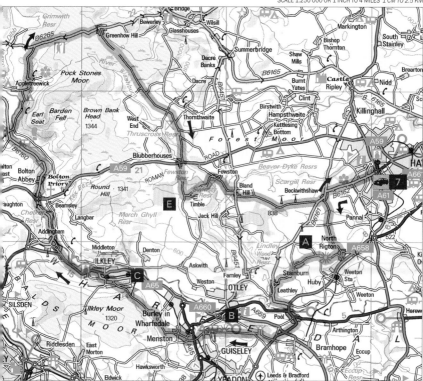

At the end of Crag Lane turn right to pass the footpath access to the crag. At the next road junction carry straight on to Stainburn. The lane twists through this delightful little hillside village where hens may be seen pecking at the verges. At the end of the village bear left to descend a 1-in-8 hill into Leathley.

Turn left at the junction with the B6161 opposite the church. This road soon meets the A658. Turn right here to join the A658 and cross the River Wharfe over Pool Bridge. Continue on the A658, forking left after the bridge, to head towards Bradford. After ¼ mile fork right when the A659 leaves to the left to Harewood. The road now climbs up Pool Bank and crosses the A660 at traffic lights opposite the Dyneley Arms pub. At the very top of the bank turn right at the crossroads on to Old Lane. At the end of this lane turn left and immediately right along York Gate which leads to The Chevin viewpoint **B**.

The view northwards over Otley and the other towns of Wharfedale is one of the highlights of this tour. There are plenty of scenic walks in the forest park. It also has a visitor centre at the White House where a Victorian farmhouse kitchen has been recreated.

Continue along The Chevin. There are views to the left over Airedale, Leeds and Bradford. This is a grand ridgeway drive.

Trollers Gill, the haunt of a barguest

39

At a T-junction follow the road to the left towards Otley and then, almost immediately, turn right, again towards Otley. This takes you to a complicated junction at The Chevin pub. Bear left on to West Chevin Road, to descend Buckle Lane. The road drops steeply to cross first the railway line and then the A65 at traffic lights.

Follow the main road through the village of Menston to reach a crossroads at the Menston Arms pub. Turn left here up Derry Hill and, at the top of the hill, turn right. Turn right again at the T-junction on to the Ilkley to Keighley road. This narrow road is very busy at times, and care is needed as it climbs up to the moor and eventually passes the Cow and Calf Hotel **C** on the right. The famous rocks can be seen on the left with a large parking area and a café. Climb up to the crags above the rocks to find yourself in a different world with Ilkley spread out below.

Continue along the road which descends steeply into Ilkley. Bear left when you meet a main road at the station. Continue along this road until it meets the A65 and then turn left. After about 2 miles turn right off the dual carriageway at Addingham, heading for Bolton Abbey. Follow the signs to the abbey around the edge of the village to join with the B6160 at its outskirts. Turn right here to pass the beautiful Farfield Hall on the left. The river is below to the right. At the A59 roundabout take the second exit to cross straight over to Bolton Abbey. Go past the Devonshire Arms Hotel on the right – Bolton Abbey car park is a little further on to the left.

The road goes through a narrow stone arch and passes behind Bolton Hall, a home of the Duke of Devonshire. The riverside car park, information centre and shop are to the right, after the

Bolton Abbey in Wharfedale

ornate Victorian drinking fountain erected in 1886 to the memory of Lord Frederick Cavendish, murdered in Phoenix Park, Dublin. A layby, a short distance further on, provides free parking.

The road continues to follow the course of the River Wharfe and there are ever-changing views of the daleside woods and pastures. At Strid Wood there is a nature trail, shop, and café. **The road then dips down to cross The Strid, a rushing torrent if the weather has been wet.** Do not take up the challenge of jumping the chasm – you may end up in the torrent and disappear in its whirlpools as a young Norman nobleman did in the twelfth century! However, it is not his ghost which haunts the spot, but that of the White Horse of Wharfedale which appears to warn of approaching death, either to the beholder or someone close to him.

After passing Barden Tower D bear right to cross the river following the road to Appletreewick and Pateley Bridge. There are parking spaces by the river, and a footpath follows it back to Bolton Abbey. **At a T-junction turn right towards Skyreholme and Pateley Bridge.** The scenery is now most spectacular with Little Simon's Seat the rocky tor on the right. **Bear left at the next junction**. Parcevall Hall can be found up the cul-de-sac to the right – the gardens of the Elizabethan mansion are open to the public. The road ends at the hall, but a lovely footpath follows the Skyreholme Beck to Trollers Gill. This is the haunt of a malevolent bear-like spirit called a barguest which used to waylay, and usually kill, lone travellers.

Follow the road up until it joins with the B6265. Turn right here towards Pateley Bridge. Stump Cross Caverns are to the right, an extensive cave system discovered by lead miners in the nineteenth century. The caverns proved to be particularly

rich in the remains of animals now extinct in Britain. The cave is open to the public and there is a shop and café.

Pass a wireless mast and then turn right immediately after this towards Harrogate. Carry straight on at the Stone House Inn crossroads. Thruscross Reservoir is to the right here – the topmost of the four reservoirs in the Washburn valley – and there is a picnic site at its southern end, about a mile down this lane.

If you do not wish to see the reservoir continue ahead along the road which reaches the A59 at Blubberhouses. There is a fine view of the Washburn valley as you come to this village, and you can see the road that the route will take climbing the other side of the valley past a little church with a spire.

Turn right on to the A59 and then immediately left to pass the church. Turn left at the crossroads at the top

of the hill **E following the sign to Timble.** There was a celebrated gang of witches in Timble in the seventeenth century. **Bear left at the next junction towards Fewston.** The road passes the Swinsty Moor car park just before it crosses over the dam which separates the Fewston and Swinsty reservoirs.

Head for Norwood by forking right when the road divides after the dam to pass Fewston church. Swinsty Reservoir in its richly-wooded setting can now be seen. There is another picnic place on the right. **After crossing over a bridge you come to the B6451. Turn right here towards Otley. After less than 1/4 mile take the road left to Beckwithshaw.** This is a high, fast moorland road with forest to the right and views left over Forest Moor. **Turn left on to the B6161 into Beckwithshaw and then, at the end of the village, turn right to return to Harrogate on the B6162.** ■

• *PLACES OF INTEREST* •

Bolton Abbey
The ruins, which stand in such a wonderfully picturesque way by the River Wharfe, are, in fact, of an Augustinian priory which was never an abbey. Many artists and writers have been inspired by the scene, amongst them Ruskin who loved seeing 'the tender decay' of the priory in association with the 'power and border sternness' of the surrounding hills.

The monastery was founded in 1151 by Alicia de Romilly, whose son was killed in attempting to jump The Strid soon afterwards. The priory was dissolved in 1539 but, unusually, part of the nave was saved to provide the parish with a church – a role it continues to serve today.

The gatehouse of the priory is incorporated into Bolton Hall, a shooting-lodge owned by the Duke of Devonshire, whose lands include much of Upper Wharfedale.

Bolton Abbey Estate. Open all year, daily, dawn to dusk. Tea shops, nature trails, fishing. Telephone: (01756) 710533.

Barden Tower
This was a hunting-lodge built in the twelfth century for the Cliffords of Skipton, administrators of Barden Forest. It was extended and enlarged by Henry, the tenth Lord Clifford (the Shepherd Lord), towards the end of the fifteenth century when the chapel and priest's house were added. He used to live here, preferring it to his commodious castle at Skipton. In 1523 he died, and it was abandoned until 1659 when Lady Anne Clifford restored it. It again became a ruin after the end of the eighteenth century when it was made roofless. Refreshment can be taken in the café which occupies the medieval priest's house, adjacent to the tower.

YORK, KNARESBOROUGH AND TADCASTER

63 MILES – 3 HOURS
START AND FINISH AT YORK

This long drive takes in many of the outstanding features of the Vale of York, which has very different scenery from that of the moors or dales – far less dramatic but with an appeal based on charming villages and wide skies. There are some grand houses to see too, such as Harewood and the lesser-known ones at Allerton and Bramham. Add to this the opportunity of exploring the lovely streets of Knaresborough and Tadcaster, plus those of York itself, and you have a very satisfying tour.

Drive out of York north-eastwards on the A19 (Thirsk road). As in most medieval cities, roads radiate from York like spokes from a wheel. **About 4 miles from the city centre, on the outskirts of the village of Shipton A, leave the main road by forking to the left, following a sign** to Beningbrough Hall and Newton-on-Ouse. Pass the Sidings Hotel which occupies a site about 20 feet (6.1 m) from the railway line.

At the T-junction which follows turn left to cross the railway. One mile further on make a turn left, again following the sign to Beningbrough Hall and Newton-on-Ouse. Please note that the first entrance to the hall is for coaches only. If you wish to visit this National Trust property use the driveway in Newton village by turning left at the green.

From Newton follow the road to Linton-on-Ouse. Continue on the road through the village to pass Linton airfield to the right. The road is lonely and hedgeless at this point as it follows the marshy land close to the river. It comes as little surprise to hear that the airfield is haunted by a ghostly airman in full flying gear – he was frequently seen when it was operated by the RAF. The River Ouse ends, for no particular reason, just to the west of Linton, at the quaintly-named Cuddy Shaw Reach, and becomes the River Ure north of this point. **When the road meets a T-junction turn left to cross Aldwark toll bridge B.** The toll only costs a few pence, and the experience of going over the rickety little bridge with a view of this lovely stretch of river is well worth the price.

At the next T-junction turn left into Little Ouseburn, crossing a graceful bridge

• PLACES OF INTEREST •

York
There are so many places to visit in this city that it is impossible to cover everything here! A section has been devoted to York in the introduction (page 13). For further information on specific places of interest contact the Tourist Information Centre at De Grey Rooms, Exhibition Square. Telephone: (01904) 621756.

Beningbrough Hall
The house dates from 1716. It is noted for the exquisite detail and quality of its interior fittings, especially the fireplaces, friezes, and door surrounds. One hundred pictures from the National Portrait Gallery are on display, and there is also outstanding furniture and porcelain.

Visitors will enjoy the exhibition devoted to servants.

There is also a well-equipped laundry and a potting shed, both Victorian.

Open April–October, Mondays–Wednesdays, Saturdays and Sundays 11–4.30. Also Fridays in July and August. Telephone: (01904) 470666.

close to the church. This is a very tranquil spot, and it is worth visiting the churchyard to see the Palladian mausoleum put up for Henry Thompson of Kirby Hall, who died in 1760. The last Thompson burial here was in 1910. The church itself dates from the fourteenth century and has a superb east window, badly damaged in 1945 when a Canadian aircraft crashed here. Note the ladder going up the inside of the tower known as a Jacob's Ladder, so dangerous that it would now be illegal to use it.

A little further on, at the next road junction, turn right to pass through the village. When you reach the B6265 turn left to Green Hammerton. Follow this busy road until it meets the A59 at Green Hammerton and then turn right towards Harrogate. As you travel along the A59 towards the A1 look to the right to catch a glimpse of the towers of Allerton Park – an enormous mansion built in Gothic Revival style.

River Nidd at Knaresborough

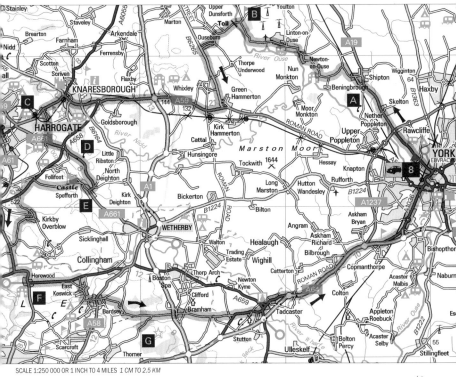

SCALE 1:250 000 OR 1 INCH TO 4 MILES *1 CM TO 2.5 KM*

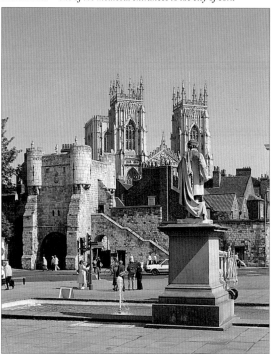

Bootham Bar – one of the medieval entrances to the city of York

to Wetherby and Calcutt. **Turn left again at the A661, Wetherby to Harrogate road, and pass Plumpton Rocks on the left D, just after the roundabout where the A661 crosses the new Harrogate relief road.** The rocks are a local beauty spot, a craggy outcrop which overlook woods and a small lake. The public can visit them on weekend and Bank Holiday afternoons.

The A661 bends sharply to the right to cross the River Crimple and enter Spofforth. After the bridge make an acute turn to the right to visit Spofforth Castle E. This magnificent ruin boasts an unusual ghost – a lady who throws herself from the battlements, but whose apparition is only ever seen from the waist up! The castle was built by Henry Percy early in the fourteenth century, more as a large fortified house than a castle. Admission is free to this English Heritage property.

Continue past the castle and then fork left towards Pannal. This is a pleasant countryside of trees and hedges.

Cross the A1 and continue to Knaresborough, bearing right to remain on the A59 when the relief road goes off to the left. Descend to the river and cross it, still on the A59, following the sign to Harrogate. **Leaving Knaresborough on this road you will pass a golf club and, after this, turn left C following the sign**

• *PLACES OF INTEREST* •

Knaresborough
The town grew up around the Anglo-Saxon castle which was erected to guard against Viking raiders sailing up the River Nidd. This was replaced by a Norman stronghold which was left derelict after the Civil War. Today the classic view of the town is dominated by the railway bridge rather than the castle – many regard this as one of the worst crimes committed against our scenery by the railway builders.

Visitors come to Knaresborough to see Mother Shipton's Cave and the Petrifying Well where everyday objects are turned to stone by the action of water rich in lime. It is said that she was born in the fifteenth century during a terrible storm in a cave close to the well.

She foretold the defeat of the Spanish Armada and warned of the Fire of London, and her other prophecies are encapsulated in the rhyme:

*Carriages without horses
 shall go,
And accidents fill the world
 with woe.
Around the world thoughts
 shall fly
In the twinkling of an eye…*

A lovely riverside walk leads to the cave.

Just below Low Bridge another famous curiosity of the town is to be found – the Chapel of Our Lady of the Crag, carved out of the cliff-face in 1409. To the right of this there is a rock figure supposed to represent St Robert of

Knaresborough, a hermit who lived in a nearby cave.

Fort Montague, above the chapel, is also partly carved from the cliff. It is a castellated, four-storey house built by Thomas Hill, a local weaver, in 1770. He was a notable eccentric who spent sixteen years building his home and gave himself a title as well as issuing his own banknotes.

Mother Shipton's Cave.
Open every day Easter–Hallowe'en 9.30–5. Hallowe'en–Easter 10–4. Telephone: (01423) 864600.
Old Courthouse Museum,
Castle Grounds. Local history exhibited in setting of a Tudor court-house.

Open May– September daily 10.30–5. Telephone: (01423) 869274.

It is flat here but there are good views. **Keep on the major road to pass a golf course and come out on to the A658. Turn left towards Poole, then after about 1 mile take the turning left to Kirkby Overblow.** This is a quiet country lane leading to a lovely village. There are wide views over Spofforth Haggs to the left. **After the Star and Garter pub turn right down Swindon Lane towards Harewood, passing the church on the right.** There are some very splendid houses along this road enjoying views over Wharfedale.

The lane comes out on to the A61. Turn left to cross a narrow bridge over the River Wharfe and then bear left to continue along the A61 to the traffic lights in the village of Harewood ⬛. If you wish to visit Harewood House turn right at the traffic lights, but to continue the route go left on to the A659 past the rows of estate cottages. The road, which was part of the grand approach to Harewood House, runs eastwards for nearly 3 miles through a straight avenue. There are four turnings off this main road all going to the next destination, the village of East Keswick. **It is probably best to pass the Traveller's Rest pub and then take the first turning to the right.**

Turn left when this lane meets with another on the edge of the village. At the main road in the centre of the village turn right. Pass two pubs, and then take the first turning left out of the village signposted to Bardsey. This village is to the right as you head straight on towards the A58 at East Rigton. **Cross straight over the main road here and drive up a steep hill following the sign to Compton and Bramham.**

Continue straight on when a lane to Compton and Collingham goes off sharply

• PLACES OF INTEREST •

Allerton Park
Large, romantic Gothic Revival country house, mainly dating from 1848, though some parts remain of the house built by the Duke of York in the late 1780s. Collections of mechanical musical intruments and vintage cars.

Open Easter–end September, Sundays and Bank Holiday Mondays 1–5. Telephone: (01423) 330927.

Harewood House
The house dates from 1759, the work of John Carr and Robert Adam, and was flamboyantly altered by Sir Charles Barry in 1843. Henry Lascelles – whose money came from collecting taxes in Barbados – moved the village eastwards out of the park (which accounts for the isolated position of the church). The interior of the house is mainly the work of Adam, and it contains original

Chippendale furniture and carpets designed by the architect. There are superbly-painted ceilings (some by Angelica Kauffmann) and panels by Antonio Zucchi. There is also Sèvres and Chinese porcelain and a collection of fine paintings. The park was landscaped by Capability Brown and contains an exotic bird garden.

Open mid-March–end October daily from 11. (Bird Garden from 10). Telephone: (01532) 886225.

Bramham Park
Beautiful Queen Anne house set in a 66-acre French baroque garden, claimed to be Versailles on a smaller scale. Museum in the old kitchens.

Open mid-June–September Tuesdays–Thursdays and Sundays 1.15–5. Telephone: (01937) 844265.

to the left. About 100 yards (91 m) further on fork left. **When you meet a more major road turn left to pass the deserted medieval village of Wothersome. At the next major road turn right. After about 1/2 mile you will reach the entrance drive to Bramham Park ⬛.** There are woodland walks, a sixty-six-acre French baroque garden (comparable to that at Hampton Court) and the house itself, a splendid Queen Anne mansion, to visit here.

After visiting Bramham Park return along the road, bearing right at the point where you joined it earlier, and cross the A1 into the village of Bramham. An embankment leads down from the main road into the village, and the view of Bramham's red-tiled roofs overlooked by the church is very picturesque. **Turn left into the village, following the signs to Bramham and Clifford. Turn right at the Red Lion and pass the war**

memorial to climb the hill with the church to the left.

Turn left at the top of the High Street and follow the signs to Stutton and Tadcaster eastwards out of the village. This road joins with the A659 to pass through the delightful town of Tadcaster. Pass John Smith's magnificent brewery on the right. The town has a fine array of Georgian buildings as well as a famous second brewery belonging to Sam Smith. The church was dismantled during 1875 to 1877 and then rebuilt on foundations 5 feet (1.5 m) higher to make it safe from floods. Close to the church the 'Virgin Viaduct' crosses the River Wharfe. It has this nickname because it was built for a railway which never reached Tadcaster.

Continue straight through the town crossing the River Wharfe and joining with the A64 (York road). This dual carriageway leads you swiftly back to the York ring road – take the A1036 to reach the city centre. ⬛

BEVERLEY AND THE HUMBER BRIDGE

44 MILES – 2 HOURS
START AND FINISH AT BEVERLEY

The tour takes you to view the longest single-span suspension bridge in the world, well, at least until the millennium when new bridges in Denmark and Japan will relegate it into third place. Certainly it makes a fine spectacle, and the walk to the southern shore and back will blow cobwebs away. The route starts from Beverley, a town full of architectural delights, and the return is on byways across the Wolds visiting a succession of lovely villages.

The village pump at Bishop Burton

From Beverley take the A164 southwards towards the Humber Bridge. You will soon see the famous windmill at Skidby on the skyline ahead. **If you wish to visit this and its museum turn right at the roundabout towards the** village, and then take the first turning left.

Continue along the A164. The 533-foot- (162 m) high towers of the bridge can be seen in the distance. **Keep straight on over the roundabout where the B1231 crosses.**

At the next roundabout turn right on to the A63. Another roundabout follows quickly. Turn acutely left here, taking the first exit and passing below the approach road to the bridge. After ¹/₂ mile turn right at a crossroads and then right again to reach the Hessle Foreshore Viewpoint **A**.

From here it is possible to drive under the bridge to reach another parking area. This is by the sail-less Hessle Whiting Mill which supplied ground-down chalk to innumerable

The spectacular Humber Bridge

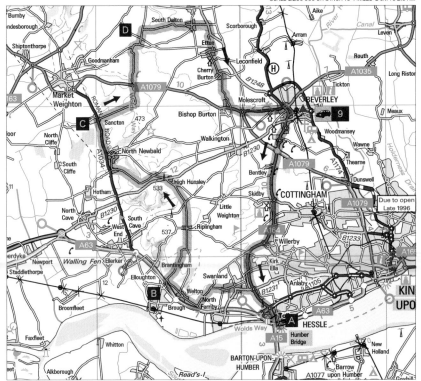

industries. Most of its machinery is preserved, and visitors may see an interesting exhibition on the occasions when it is open in the summer. From here go back and, for a different viewpoint, visit the Humber Bridge Country Park on the western side of the approach road where there are refreshments.

Return to the roundabout on the A164 and turn right towards Hull. At the next roundabout, which follows in ½ mile, turn left to keep on the A164. At the following roundabout turn left on to the B1231 to the village of Swanland. At a T-junction turn right into the centre of the village. After 200 yards (183 m) turn left into West End which takes you out of Swanland.

There are views of an enormous quarry face (claimed to be the largest in Britain) as the lane bears left to pass the quarries and reach Welton. **At the traffic lights, confusingly, Melton is**

• PLACES OF INTEREST •

Beverley

This town is one of the most beautiful in Britain with a host of marvellous buildings, many of them Georgian. The minster is grander than many a cathedral, but St Mary's Church is also outstanding, and some experts consider it to be the most beautiful parish church in England. However, most people know St Mary's for the carving of a jolly rabbit on a doorway which is supposed to have inspired Lewis Carroll with the character for *Alice in Wonderland*. Even more lively is the painted group of minstrels that may be seen on one of the capitals. They appear there because they paid for that particular pillar in the sixteenth century. There are amusing carvings in the minster too, in the sixty-eight misericords, where medieval craftsmen have portrayed men and beasts in amusing situations – there are even two woodcarvers quarrelling.

Beverley, as befits an ancient market town, is also famed for its shops which offer merchandise hard to find elsewhere. There are gunsmiths and saddlers as well as delicatessens specialising in a delicious range of locally-produced food. A lot of the shops appeal specially to country people, and many of these visit Beverley for the horseracing. Its racecourse claims to be the friendliest course in the north of England, holding about eighteen flat meetings each year. A final attraction must be the unique Museum of Army Transport which features exhibits ranging from Field Marshall Montgomery's Rolls Royce to the only three-wheels-in-line motorcycle.

Museum of Army Transport, Flemingate. Two indoor halls house exhibits of army road, rail, sea and air transport. Open all the year except Christmas, daily 10–5. Telephone: (01482) 860445.

47

Beverley Minster, grander than many cathedrals

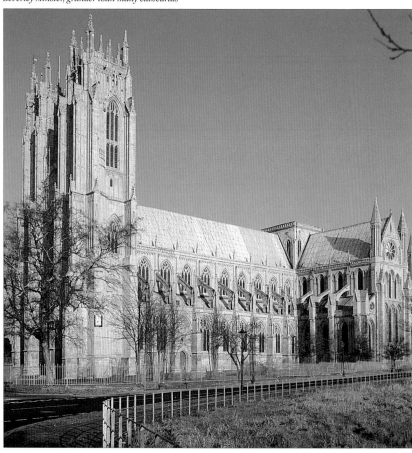

to the left and Welton to the right. **Turn right to Welton.** The highwayman Dick Turpin is supposed to have been captured at the Green Dragon Inn here.

There is a one-way system round the very large church with its massive central tower. The church was drastically restored by Sir George Gilbert Scott in 1862, but in compensation there is stained glass by William Morris and Sir Edward Burne-Jones. **Turn right at the T-junction beyond the church.** This is a picturesque street with a stream and attractive cottages. **At the end of the green turn left towards Beverley. At the next junction go straight ahead to Elloughton Hill.** There is a tremendous view here over the Humber and the flat land beyond, and it makes a good

place to have a picnic.

Turn right at the T-junction into Elloughton Dale B. The road climbs steadily up this beautifully-wooded dale and joins with the Wolds Way at the top. **Follow the surfaced road round to the right. Turn left at a T-junction on to a straight road which heads northwards along the crest of the Wolds.** There are wide views to the right. **Go straight over at the crossroads towards Walkington and Beverley.** As you come to the next crossroads there are towers in the fields which were the airshafts of a tunnel on a disused railway. **Again go straight over the crossroads.** The road remains very straight, but undulating, passing through large fields of grain, sugar-beet, potatoes etc.

Turn left at a T-junction towards Newbald and Market Weighton. The wireless masts ahead show that this must be one of the highest points on the Wolds. **Cross straight over the B1230 and, at the next unsignposted crossroads, go left on to an unfenced road.** There are outstanding views from here. This part of the route is shared with the Wolds Way. It looks as though most of southern Yorkshire is spread out before you – the power stations at Selby and Ferrybridge are prominent landmarks. The road dips down into a lovely valley before South Newbald.

Bear right along the village street which joins South and North Newbald. You will pass the magnificent Norman church. **Turn right at a T-junction,**

and then bear left round the village green following signs to Market Weighton. At the A1034 turn right. There is a Shire Horse Centre at Flower Hill Farm, about 2 miles to the north-east of North Newbald.

The next village is Sancton **C**. Turn right just as you enter the village on to a well-concealed byway called Beverley Lane. If you reach the Star pub then you have missed this turn! This single track road climbs back to the top of the Wolds where the landscape is spread out, treeless and hedgeless. It crosses the A1079 and remains narrow with broad verges. You will not meet much traffic on this byway. The enormous fields and the wide distances make the scattered dwellings look like dolls' houses.

Turn right at the next T-junction to pass under a high and handsome brick railway bridge. About 1/2 mile further on there is a welcome car park and tearoom at the disused Kiplingcotes Station. A railway

footpath uses the old trackbed to link Beverley with Market Weighton. It is named The Hudson Way after the famous railway magnate who lived at nearby Londesborough. Kiplingcotes is famous for being the venue of the Kiplingcotes Derby, Britain's oldest horserace, which has been held since 1519. It takes place on the third Thursday in March.

Take the turn opposite the station entrance **D** which goes north towards Middleton-on-the-Wolds. After about 1 mile turn right on to South Dalton Park Road. The grass in the centre of this lane shows it is not used by much traffic. This too is a delightful byway which crosses a cattle-grid into a magnificent park. Take the left fork when the road divides. The right-hand road goes to Dalton Hall, the ancestral home of Lord Hotham, which may be glimpsed through the trees. The road emerges into an estate village of whitewashed houses. The

Victorian church is to the left. It has a slender tower and spire and its weathervane is 200 feet (61 m) above ground level.

Turn right, and then immediately left in the middle of the village, and pass by a large pond. At the unsignposted crossroads turn right. You are now on the B1248 heading towards Beverley. Very soon after this turn right again following a sign to South Wolds School. This lane leads into Etton. The wall by the side of the road leans at an alarming angle! Turn right to pass the church and then left towards Cherry Burton. At the crossroads in this village go straight over following the sign to Bishop Burton.

It is worth diverting to see this lovely village by turning right when the lane meets the A1079.

From the village turn back down the A1079 and then on to the A1035 to return to Beverley past the racecourse. ■

• PLACES OF INTEREST •

Skidby Windmill and Museum
A complete working windmill with a museum related to corn production and milling. The mill was built in 1821. Café. Telephone for dates when the sails will turn.
Open October–Easter Monday–Friday 10–4. Easter–October Tuesday–Saturday 10–4, Sundays 1.30–4. Telephone: (01482) 883919.

Humber Bridge
The statistics are stunning – there are 90 acres of paintwork, 30,000 tons of steel wire, the anchorage points on the southern shore weigh 300,000 tons – and the bridge has never been able to pay its way since its opening in 1981. Yet it must be worth a great deal as an attraction for tourists, even though one is left wondering whether the old paddle-steamers, which used to ply across the

Humber, would not attract even more interest if they were to be resurrected.

Northern Shire Horse Centre
Flower Hill Farm, North Newbald. Shire horses, harness room, horse-drawn vehicles, vintage tractors and threshing machine. Rare animals.
Open Easter Sunday–end September Mondays–Thursdays, Sundays 10–5. Telephone: (01430) 827270.

Bishop Burton
This is a 'chocolate-box' village with a pond in front of the church and many beautiful cottages. Its war memorial is in the centre of the pond, and on the edge is a strange pump once used by villagers as their water supply. John Wesley used to preach here beneath a great wych-elm on the

green, but the tree toppled after being struck by lightning in 1836. Generously, the squire used a piece of its wood and had a likeness of Wesley carved from it. He presented this to the new Wesleyan Chapel, and it stayed there until a declining congregation led to its demise at the turn of the century. The bust was auctioned and bought by the Anglican vicar who paid for it with thirty silver threepenny bits, and then mocked the Methodists for selling their leader for thirty pieces of silver. Anyway, the result is that Wesley's bust is now proudly displayed in the parish church. Bishop Burton is also famed for once having fielded a cricket team which comprised ten Ducks and a Swann, the Ducks being a large local family who were joiners and wheelwrights and Swann being the village schoolmaster.

POCKLINGTON, WHARRAM PERCY AND SLEDMERE

47 MILES – 2 HOURS
START AND FINISH AT POCKLINGTON

This route is designed to give the motorist a flavour of the Wolds – the area of the East Riding where the scenery often rivals that of the Moors or Dales, albeit with a softer character. Moreover, it has a succession of lovely villages, the best of them comparable with the showplaces further north and many with the same characteristics. Stone-built cottages are usually grouped attractively about the church and overlook a broad green and pond. Two places of particular interest feature in the route – Wharram Percy, the most romantic of lost medieval villages, and Sledmere, its estate village surrounding the mansion, a treasure-house which, more than any other, retains a special lived-in atmosphere.

• PLACES OF INTEREST •

Pocklington

Pocklington is one of the lesser-known treasures of Yorkshire – a small market town situated on the edge of the Vale of York with the Wolds rising up steeply to the east. The church has a magnificent Perpendicular tower which gives it the nickname of 'Cathedral of the Wolds'. In 1733 Thomas Pelling was killed when he fell from the tower on to the battlements of the choir. He was known as 'The Flying Man' and had rigged up apparatus which should have seen him land in the grounds of a pub below. Unfortunately, when he began abseiling down the tower a rope came loose and he dropped to his death.

Pocklington has elegant houses, many of them Georgian, overlooking little triangular greens which are unaccountably called 'squares'. One of the finest Georgian houses, Oak House on the Market Place, was converted into the Ritz cinema which is now Penny Arcadia.

Penny Arcadia. Collection of penny-in-the-slot amusements, including 'What the Butler Saw' and self-playing musical instruments. Guided tours and demonstrations. Café.
Open May and September daily 12.30– 5, June–August daily 10–5. Telephone: (01759) 303420 or (01377) 217248.

Burnby Hall, on the south-east outskirts of Pocklington. This was the home of Major Stewart who bequeathed the house with its grounds and contents to the town.

Its lake has the most comprehensive collection of water lilies in Europe – there are some eighty varieties in total. Children enjoy feeding the giant fish in the lake and seeing the stuffed animals and other trophies brought back by Major Stewart.

Open April–September daily 10–6. October–March weekdays 10–4. Telephone: (01262) 676316.

From Pocklington church take the B1246 (Driffield road) out of the town. After 1 1/2 miles turn left **A** following a sign to Kilnwick Percy. There is a glimpse of the hall to the right – it has an imposing portico with Ionic columns and dates from the late-eighteenth century. It now serves as a Buddhist centre. The restored Norman church stands in the parkland just to the south of the church and is reached by a footpath from the main road.

The lane continues across open fields, the views improving all the time. There are hedges again as it descends into Millington. **Turn right at a T-junction and follow the lane through the village to a crossroads. Turn right again here following the sign to Millington Pastures and Huggate, unless you wish to visit the unspoilt Norman church which is a few yards to the left.**

The route continues into Millington Dale. It zig-zags down to the entrance to

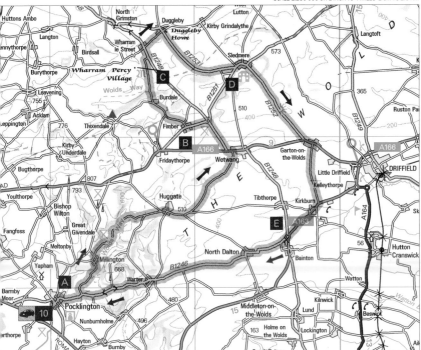

Millington Wood where there is a car park and picnic site. The wood belongs to the council and is a Site of Special Scientific Interest, being the last remaining area of Wolds Ash woodland. You can walk through the wood from here or take one of the innumerable footpaths which cross the dale. One of these is the Roman road which leads from Brough to Malton. The site of the lost Roman town of Delgovicia is supposed to lie close to the entrance to Millington Wood.

The road climbs up the dale, following its gentle curves – several more inviting footpaths lead up side dales to the left and right. **At the top of the dale the lane meets with another – bear left to join this and continue into Huggate.** The main part of the village is to the left of the main road. **Pass the Wolds Inn and about 1 mile after this fork left to Wetwang.** The road is still on top of the wolds and gives wonderfully extensive vistas. **At the A166, just outside Wetwang, turn left and then right on to the**

B1248 towards Malton. When this road reaches a round-about turn left on to the B1251. There is a picnic site with toilets here.

After about 1 mile turn right B at Fimber, following a sign to Burdale and Thixendale. This lovely lane descends steeply passing a turn on the right to Towthorpe. The narrow single-track lane winds its way up the dale with a disused railway line to the right. **Bear right when the road to Fridaythorpe leaves to the left, and bear right again by a pond to leave the Thixendale**

Wharram Percy – a lost village of the Wolds

51

road, now following the sign to Wharram le Street. About 1¼ miles after this point a track goes off to the left to the car park for the Wharram Percy medieval village site **C**. This was one of hundreds of hitherto prosperous villages which were deserted at the end of the Middle Ages. The popular belief that such places were abandoned because of epidemics of plague has been shown to be erroneous and, in the case of Wharram Percy, the reason for its decline lies in its landlords evicting tenant farmers to make room for sheep. If you walk down to the village by the footpath you will find a ruined medieval church standing amongst the remains of the thirty

---

• PLACES OF INTEREST •

The Wolds Landscape and Flora

The chalk wolds of East Yorkshire are at their most dramatic around Pocklington. Here the western escarpment rises steeply to the north east of the town and is scored by narrow dry valleys. These are too steep for cultivation and are usually kept for sheep, just as they were in late medieval times when landlords swept away peasant smallholders and made a vast sheep-run out of the upland wolds. Footpaths run through several of the loveliest of the dales. Walkers can appreciate wild flowers unique to chalk country like bloody cranesbill, burnet saxifrage and the pyramidal orchid. The marshy ground in the valley bottom is often colonised by marsh marigold, and watercress if there is a spring nearby. Millington Dale, about 4 miles to the north-east of Pocklington, is the finest of these valleys. It is a Site of Special Scientific Interest, especially important because the flora thrives undisturbed. Horsedale, 2 miles north of Huggate, is another lovely dale, easily accessible by footpath from this route, where harebells, rock roses, and autumn gentians may be found.

Sledmere

The house dates from 1751 when Richard Sykes laid the foundation-stone of a new house to replace the medieval manor which had previously stood here. In 1776 the house came to Sir Christopher Sykes, the agricultural reformer who was a pioneer in returning the Wolds, at the time a vast sheep run, to arable farming. Sir Christopher began by engaging Capability Brown to landscape the grounds, which entailed moving the village out of sight of the mansion. With this accomplished, he turned his attention to enlarging the house. This was done mainly to his own designs, though he consulted two famous architects of his day, John Carr of York and Samuel Wyatt. The interior owes much to Joseph Rose, the celebrated plasterer who became a friend of Sir Christopher and influenced the furnishing of the rooms as well as their decoration. This house remained virtually unaltered until a terrible fire destroyed much of it in 1911 (fortunately the fire was slow to gain a hold and nearly all of the valuable contents were moved outside). This resulted in much of it being rebuilt in Edwardian style during the years of the Great War. Sledmere remains in the hands of the Sykes family, and visitors will find it a particularly friendly house as well as a fascinating one.

Sledmere House. Open Easter, May–third week in September Tuesdays–Thursdays, Saturdays and Sundays 1.30–5. Telephone: (01377) 236208 or 236231.

or so homesteads which once comprised the community. The spot is immeasurably beautiful and has a romantic atmosphere unlike any other. The second part of its name derives from one of its Lords of the Manor – the Percy family – whose principal seat is at Alnwick in Northumberland.

Return to the lane and go left to descend to the B1248. Turn left on to this and then right at the crossroads at Wharram le Street. Just a little further along the main road from this junction is the Red House which provides refreshments. **The lane leads to the village of Duggleby where you turn right on to the B1253 towards Sledmere and Driffield.** This stretch of road is characterised by enormous hedgeless fields. As you approach the Sledmere estate the landscape becomes more wooded.

Turn left on to the B1253 opposite an ornate memorial. Follow the road round

Milk-churn gate-post near Huggate, one of many in the district made by Italian POWs

past the Triton Inn and the entrance to Sledmere House . **Keep straight on at the next junction, taking the B1252 towards Driffield.** This road again follows high ground as it heads south-eastwards and passes the needle-like monument to Sir Tatton Sykes. **Bear left**

when you join the A166 again. **Take the first turning to the right at the centre of Garton-on-the-Wolds, signposted to Kirkburn.** Pass the church, which has outstanding Norman stonework on the archway to the west door, but is dark and gloomy inside with Victorian frescoes which were liked by Pevsner. **This road leads to the A163. Turn right here to pass through the village of Kirkburn. At a roundabout** , **on the outskirts of Bainton, continue straight ahead on the B1246. Take this road to pass through North Dalton and continue on the B1246 to the village of Warter.** Here there is a church containing interesting memorials. Warter is an estate village owned by the Guinness family and has lovely thatched cottages. The road then climbs up to the top of the wolds again to give a grand finale of a view over the Vale of York with Pocklington in the distance. ■

Millington Pasture, a little-known beauty spot

BRONTË COUNTRY

42 MILES – 2½ HOURS
START AND FINISH AT HEBDEN BRIDGE

This tour takes you on a literary pilgrimage to Haworth, the town where the Brontë family lived and worked. The route crosses lovely moorland and passes through small spinning and weaving villages of Calderdale, such as Booth, with typical dark stone cottages. It trespasses into Lancashire to visit beautiful Wycoller, which also has Brontë associations to enhance its romance. Be warned, there are steep and narrow sections of road on this route, particularly towards the end!

Widdop Gate – a favourite spot for picnics

From Hebden Bridge Tourist Information Centre, opposite the post office, take the A646 westwards and then the first major turning to the right. Because this turn is so acute it means, in effect, turning left off the main road, just after Bankfoot Garage, and using a specially-made loop road in order to make the right turn to Heptonstall, Slack and Colden. **Keep on the major road bearing right towards Slack.** You are soon high up above Hebden Bridge on the side of the narrow valley. Calderdale is very different from the dales to the north, and this can be appreciated from here. The valley and its tributaries, known as 'cloughs', were adopted by industry in the eighteenth and nineteenth centuries for the power provided by their rushing waters. Mills were established by the streams, but housing for the workers had to occupy less valuable sites on the steep hillsides above, and this lead to the characteristic top-and-bottom houses where two dwellings occupied one site.

Slack is a village with a wide street of the usual stone houses. **Fork right at the end of this village towards Widdop and Colne.** The road climbs up

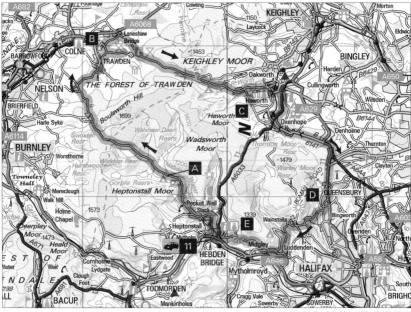

SCALE 1:250 000 OR 1 INCH TO 4 MILES 1 CM TO 2.5 KM

Hebden Bridge

The town grew up around the bridging-point over Hebden Water. Its pack-horse-bridge, dating from 1510, was an important part of the route from Burnley to Halifax. With the birth of the Industrial Revolution the power of Hebden Water and the River Calder was harnessed. Weaving and spinning mills became established and workers (often peasants dispossessed of their small-holdings by the Acts of Enclosure) came to the valley to work in them. 'Top-and-bottom' houses were built to accommodate them. This was an economical form of dwelling erected where the land was steep, so that two families could occupy one site.

The Rochdale Canal, and then the railway, were built alongside the river to link the towns of Calderdale. The textile industry has drastically declined leaving a host of redundant buildings, and much of the town's appeal today lies in the way these have been put to use. Even the canal is now a tourist attraction, and you may care to have a horse-drawn trip in a barge. Following the town trail is the best way to learn more about Hebden Bridge.

Walkley's Clogs, Burnley Road. Famous for its clog-making business. Now expanded to be the centre-piece of a collection of Victorian-style shops selling good Yorkshire produce. Craftsmen can usually be seen making them. Restaurant. Open daily. Telephone: (01422) 842061.

Automobilia, Billy Lane, Old Town. This is a vintage car and transport museum where you can actually hire out an 'inheritance car' if you wish to do the tour in style! Open April–September Tuesdays–Fridays 10–5. Saturdays and Sundays 12–5. October, November and March Saturdays and Sundays 12–5. December– February Sundays only 12–5. Telephone: (01422) 844775.

World of the Honey Bee, Hebble End Mill. A museum showing bees at work and how honey is made. Open daily 10.30–5.30. Afternoons in winter. Telephone: (01422) 845557.

The Hebden Crypt. A chamber of horrors sure to appeal to children. Open March–October Tuesdays–Sundays 10–5. Telephone: (0422) 845690

Wycoller Hall

The hall was built in the late sixteenth century and extended a century later by Squire Henry Owen Cunliffe in the hope of attracting a wealthy heiress. He was a rumbustious character who could have been invented by Henry Fielding. The squire was deeply in debt when he died in 1819, watching a cockfight from his deathbed. Not surprisingly his

ghost haunts Wycoller as does Guytrash Lightfoot, a fearsome spectral dog which is a portent of death and is described by Charlotte Brontë in *Jane Eyre*. She based 'Ferndean Hall' on Wycoller, and a plate of the hall illustrated an 1898 edition of the novel. At this time, although the house was empty, it was still reasonably intact. The lovely pack-horse bridge at Wycoller is known as 'Sally's bridge', after Squire Cunliffe's mother, Sally Owen. An Interpretation Centre occupies the seventeenth-century barn next to the ruins of the hall.

to the top of the hill where there is a National Trust car park on the right – Clough Hole – which overlooks the wooded valley. Here there is access to Hardcastle Crags (National Trust) via a footpath leading down to the bottom of the valley and then over a footbridge. The crags overlook two steep, wooded valleys threaded by a labyrinth of footpaths. It is one of the last habitats of our native red squirrel.

Soon after this the road passes a caravan site and then descends steeply to Widdop Gate . The riverside is a favourite venue with picnickers and a good starting point for walks. There is parking at the top

Haworth Parsonage – home of the Brontë family

Haworth

In 1820 Patrick and Maria Brontë and their six children moved into the Parsonage at Haworth. Patrick was destined to be the longest-serving rector of Haworth, serving the parish for forty-one years and outliving all of his children. He came from Ireland with the surname Brunty, but changed this in admiration of Lord Nelson, who took the name Brontë when he was made a peer.

When Patrick Brontë began his ministry Haworth was a busy village with its occupants either employed in the local mills or working at home on hand looms. The very long mullioned upstairs windows of the outworkers' cottages can still be seen in buildings lining Main Street. They were built this way to afford as much light as possible.

Today Haworth seems a healthy place, a hilltop village full of fresh air. However, in the Brontë's time few households could afford adequate heating, and the main water supply was badly polluted. In 1850 the average age of death was twenty-five with nearly half the children dying before the age of six. It seems miraculous that, unlike their sisters, Emily, Charlotte and Anne survived long enough to write the works of genius which we enjoy to this day.

Most visitors to Haworth will want to visit the Parsonage Museum and the church (though most of this was rebuilt after the death of Patrick Brontë), explore the cobbled streets of the village (many of the shops sell craftworks produced locally) and, perhaps, wander up to the moors where the famous sisters found so much inspiration.

Brontë Parsonage Museum, Church Street. Manuscripts and wide-ranging memorabilia of the Brontës in the small house furnished as in the days when it was occupied by the family.

Open April–September daily 10–5 October–March daily 11–4.30. Closed at Christmas and 10 January–4 February (approximately). Telephone: (01535) 642323.

Keighley and Worth Valley Railway. Steam trains run on the 5-mile track from Keighley to Oxenhope and there is a station at Haworth. Under-cover collection of engines and carriages at Oxenhope.

Open all year Saturdays and Sundays 9–5.30. Easter Week, Christmas Week, Spring Bank Holiday–first week in September daily 11.30–5.30. Telephone: (01535) 645214.

Haworth Museum of Childhood, 117 Main Street. A fascinating collection of toys, dolls, and games. Working toy trains. Open Easter–31 October daily. Telephone for times: (01535) 643593.

The Brontë Weaving Shed. Working water-wheel, hand looms and an exhibition devoted to Timmy Feather, the last of the Yorkshire hand-loom weavers. Telephone: (01535) 646217

---

of the hill before the Pack Horse Inn which stands 975 feet (297 m) above sea-level. These moors are the catchment area for a chain of reservoirs, and the road passes close to one of them, Widdop Reservoir. The parking place at the upper end affords a good view back. The county boundary is at the top of the pass, and you are in Lancashire as the view to the north opens up and the road begins to dip down. Pendle Hill can be clearly seen ahead, slightly to the left. There is a steep descent and an unguarded precipice to the right. **Keep to the right when this road goes off to the left. The road climbs once more to reach a junction. Turn right here towards Colne and pass Coldwell Reservoir. After this a road to Nelson forks off the left. Keep ahead here on the major road and, at the crossroads that follows, turn right. After passing Trawden**

church bear left to go through the village following the sign towards Wycoller Country Park. Pass the post office and then take a turning to the right B also signposted to the country park. After ¹/₂ mile a further turn to the right takes you to the car park. Wycoller village lies in a cul-de-sac, and visitors are encouraged to leave their cars in the car park just above it and walk down to the beauty spot.

Return from the car park and turn right at the first junction. Turn right again at the second junction following the sign to Laneshaw Bridge. In this hamlet you will cross a small bridge before coming to a T-junction. Turn right here, away from the main bridge, on to the Haworth road. After just 1 mile there is another country park car park which gives a more picturesque, and more energetic, access to

Wycoller for walkers who are prepared to make the steep climb back. The views are superb from here but get even better as you proceed along this road. The road passes two reservoirs and tearooms at Scar Top, perhaps the highest in England. **Bear right here and descend steeply past Ponden Reservoir.** It is said that the navvies who worked here in the 1870s were so badly victualled that local boys sold them earthworms to eat. The reservoirs harness the streams which were originally the source of the River Worth. There is a craft centre and tearoom at Ponden Mill.

The road then passes the famous Old Silent Inn on the right – it takes its name from having hidden Bonnie Prince Charlie after the 1745 uprising. It is also famous for the ghost of a former landlady which is supposed to ring a little bell, just as the landlady did in her lifetime, to call stray cats to the back door for

The Brontë Memorial Chapel in the parish church at Haworth

feeding. **Turn right, ¼ mile past the Wuthering Heights free house, on to the Oxenhope road (also signposted to Penistone Hill Country Park) and cross the dam wall of the Lower Laithe Reservoir.** The car park on Penistone Hill **C** is a wonderful viewpoint for the Brontë country, and a good starting point for walks across the moorland beloved by the novelists. **Return over the dam to the main road and turn right to drive down into Haworth.** There are many places where you can park to visit this interesting town.

The tour continues through the town on the main road past the Bygone Days Museum. **Cross the railway bridge and immediately turn right to climb the steep Brow Road which takes you up to the A6033. Turn right on to this and follow it for about 1½ miles into Oxenhope. Take the Denholme road here by turning left on to the B6141 and pass another reservoir before meeting with the A629 just outside the village. Turn right towards Halifax. Keep on the A629 for about 2 miles, passing the Rock Hollow Tearooms on the right, and then the Moorlands Inn on the left. Two hundred yards (61 m) past the latter turn right D into a concealed road (Per Lane).**

The road drops down to meet a major road. **Turn sharply to the right here and descend to the valley and then pass Mixenden Reservoir. The road goes straight over two mini roundabouts. Follow the main road round to the right at Moor End Road climbing quite steeply to come to a crossroads. A pleasant diversion here is to turn right and climb up to Ovenden Moor.** There is an impressive wind farm here. This is a good starting point for walks in Calderdale.

If you do not take this diversion go straight over the crossroads and then take the turning on the left (Bank House Lane) to Booth and Luddenden. This lane goes down steeply but gives tremendous views. At Booth the streets are cobbled and the village is very picturesque. **After a steep climb past Murgatroyd's abandoned mill turn right towards Midgley Old Town and Pecket Well.** The tour does not go to the picturesque village of Luddenden as it lacks a car park. However, a keen Brontë-follower will wish to visit it since Branwell was a paid-up member of the pub's library. This was in 1841 when he was ticket-clerk at Luddenden Foot Station, at the bottom of the valley. There are a few parking spaces at the Lord Nelson pub which can be found next to the church. At the top of the hill above the village is White Rock, a boulder painted white on May Day morning each year to propitiate the spirit of a long-dead chieftain who is said to lie underneath.

Midgley has a very effective traffic-calming scheme using cobbled bumps. A low stone wall guards a precipitous drop to the left, and there is a wonderful view of the valley from here. **A golf course is to the right as you come up to the Mount Skip Inn E. Bear left here down Wadsworth Lane to descend steeply into Hebden Bridge.** ■

Hebden Bridge from Midgley

SKIPTON AND GRASSINGTON

45 MILES – 2½ HOURS
START AND FINISH AT SKIPTON

Skipton is a bustling market town which seems just as busy today as it did in the days before its bypass was built. Its castle guards the Aire Gap where two important trans-Pennine roads meet. This route crosses the moors from Skipton to Wharfedale and visits Burnsall and Grassington, two of the prettiest villages in the Dales. The return is by country lanes which, at one point, run by the Leeds-Liverpool Canal, perhaps the finest engineering achievement of the eighteenth century.

Skipton is often hailed as 'the Gateway to the Dales', though in reality it stands at the threshold of Airedale before the river drops to Keighley, Bradford and Leeds. However, there is easy access from here into Ribblesdale and Wharfedale, so this may be forgiven in terms of practicality if not geography.

Head up Skipton's High Street to the mini-roundabout by the war memorial and take the right exit to follow the A59 (Harrogate road). At the top of the hill take the turning to the left to Embsay. The road goes beneath the bypass and then a railway bridge to reach the village. The steam railway is a major attraction here. The track of the old Skipton-Ilkley railway has been relaid for 2½ miles eastwards from Embsay to Holywell Halt, and there is a collection of fourteen locomotives and historic rolling stock.

Keep on the main road through Embsay. At the outskirts of the village take the turn left to Eastby and Barden to pass the church on the left. Eastby is a small village overlooked to the north by limestone crags. The road passes over a cattle-grid and after this there is a parking area which allows the extensive moorland views to be enjoyed. The Lower Barden Reservoir is ahead as the road begins to snake down into Upper Wharfedale. **Bear left when you meet the B6160 to pass Barden Tower.** Refreshments are available here (as they are at a farmhouse a little further along the road). **Keep on the B6160 to pass, but not to cross, Barden Bridge.**

The road runs high up on the side of the valley with grand views over Upper Wharfedale. As the road begins a 1-in-5 descent

Skipton
This is a market town in the very best sense, there seems to be a market here every day of the week, attracting people from near and far to buy the goods on offer – from fresh food to exotic clothing and furnishing from the Far East. It also has a modern shopping arcade and the usual supermarkets.

The castle has overlooked these goings-on since the time of the Conquest from its position at the top of the High Street. It came into the possession of the Clifford family in 1309, and they rebuilt the Norman castle to make it a mighty medieval stronghold. Its defences were put to the test during the Civil War when its garrison withstood Cromwell's siege for three years before being starved out. Cromwell left the castle a ruin, but Lady Anne Clifford rebuilt it in the years after 1650, adding comfortable living quarters to the surviving medieval defence-works. That is how we see it today – the old

work wonderfully-blended with the new.

Skipton's heritage as a market town and an important textile centre is illustrated in the exhibits of the Craven Museum which also encompasses other aspects of history in the district, such as lead mining.

The parish church was damaged during the Civil War siege, but has a grand west tower with battlements and pinnacles, and its interior is impressive with excellent brasses and a magnificent Jacobean font-cover.
Skipton Castle. Open all year daily 10–6 except October– February 10–4. Sundays from 2. Telephone: (01756) 792442.

Craven Museum, Town Hall, High Street. Open April– September Mondays Wednesdays–Saturdays 10–5. Sundays 2–5. October– March Mondays, Wednesdays–Fridays 2–5. Saturdays 10–4.30. Sundays 2–5. Telephone: (01756) 794079.

into Burnsall there is a classic view of the village, with its bridge and church nestling in the bottom of the valley **A**. **Keep on the main road through Burnsall to pass the post office.** There is a very interesting church here.

At Threshfield you come to a road junction where you turn right to cross the River Wharfe into Grassington **B**. This is the most famous of the villages in Wharfedale. The main car park is by the Dales Park Centre and there is, unfortunately, little available elsewhere.

Return over the bridge to Threshfield, pass the road you came up earlier and turn left on to the B6265 to Skipton. The road passes a large quarry to the right before the village of Cracoe. **At the end of the village a road goes off to the right signposted Hetton and Gargrave. Take this to cross the Dales railway and come into Hetton. Keep on the main road to pass the Angel Inn and then turn right to Airton and Winterburn.** This is part of the Yorkshire Dales Cycle Way, a typical dales lane –

The Upper Wharfedale Museum, Grassington

narrow and tortuous.

At Winterburn, turn right off the Gargrave road over a narrow humpbacked bridge, towards Calton and Airton. Calton was the home of 'Honest' John Lambert, one of Cromwell's officers who managed to escape execution when Charles II was restored to the throne – he was banished to Guernsey instead. At Calton the road drops steeply to cross the River Aire and the

Pennine Way and enter Airton. A cottage stands on the triangular green here, its garden enclosed by a stone wall. This is a seventeenth-century squatter's house and must have caused the village much controversy when it was built on the common land. Airton had an important linen industry, the first mill being erected by William Ellis, a Quaker who spent some time preaching in America before returning to Yorkshire.

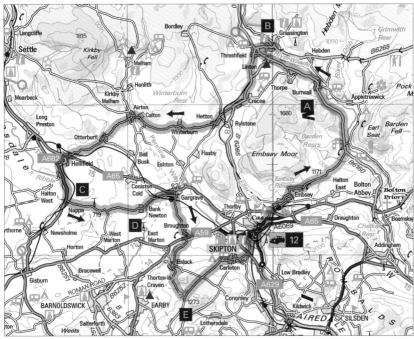

SCALE 1:250 000 OR 1 INCH TO 4 MILES *1 CM TO 2.5 KM*

59

One of the loveliest canal scenes in the country – the Leeds-Liverpool Canal at Bank Newton

He also built the lovely Friends' Meeting House in 1700 and lived in the house opposite. WAE is carved on the lintel – the 'A' standing for Alice, William's wife.

Go straight over the crossroads at the centre of Airton towards Otterburn and Hellifield. This is a twisting country lane with hedges, as well as stone walls, and fields of pasture on each side. **Beyond Otterburn the road runs close to the railway line and crosses it just before Hellifield to join the A65.** Hellifield was important in the days of steam railways for having the 'shed' that many of the crews belonged to who worked the Settle-Carlisle line. The banking engines that waited by the steepest parts of the line ready to give expresses or heavy goods trains help over the summit were based here. **Turn right to pass the church and then left by the Black Horse pub to cross under another railway bridge. At the T-junction turn left on to the A682 towards Gisburn.**

After about 2 miles look for a turning **C** at the top of a small rise which goes to Gargrave. This turning is easily missed. Look for a height restriction sign which gives an indication of where to turn. The road climbs steadily towards the radio masts at the top of the hill. **At a road junction turn left towards Gargrave and come to the hamlet of Bank Newton D.** The road runs next to the Leeds-Liverpool Canal. This was the most difficult part of the canal to build and was the last section to be opened in 1790. Look for parking places by the canal and walk along the tow path to view the flight of six locks which takes the canal up from

A classic Wharfedale landscape – the church and bridge at Burnsall

Burnsall

Situated at the end of the village St Wilfred's Church probably stands on the site of a Saxon church. It was completely rebuilt in the sixteenth century (a plaque says it was further 'butified' in 1612). Several interesting relics from the earlier church can be seen.

Burnsall Grammar School is to the south of the church and was built in 1602 by Sir William Craven, whose story reads a little like that of Dick Whittington. Born in the neighbouring village of Appletreewick (in one of the two cottages which were later joined together to make the village chapel), he was apprenticed by his parents into the drapery trade in London. Immensely successful in this, he was knighted and, in 1611, made Lord Mayor of London. His son, also William, married the sister of Charles I and was created the first Earl of Craven (the name was also that of a Saxon kingdom based on Skipton).

Grassington

Although Grassington is usually considered to be a village, it boasts a town hall. It is a lovely place whatever its status, centred on a cobbled square surrounded by old buildings with narrow lanes radiating from it.

The railway had a short life here, the branch line being extended from Skipton in 1901 and closing in 1930. This was, however, enough time to establish Grassington as a tourist centre, which was just as well since its traditional lead mining and textile industries were in decline. Most of its cottages date from the time of the lead mines – there is one at the top of Garrs Lane called Theatre Cottage. This was converted from a barn which served as a theatre in the heyday of the lead mines and attracted famous actors like Edmund Kean.

Grassington's earlier history was chequered. The neighbourhood has a wealth of Iron Age hill-forts and Bronze Age tumuli which show that the surrounding moors were popular with prehistoric settlers. Its bridge is medieval and was built when the village was being ravaged by frequent Scottish raids. It was also unfortunate in losing a quarter of its inhabitants to the Black Death in 1349. Perhaps this is why it lacks the medieval church which might be expected here.

Upper Wharfedale Museum, The Square. A comprehensive collection of artefacts illustrating life here through the ages. The museum is situated in a beautiful eighteenth-century cottage.

Open Easter–October daily 2–4.30, October–Easter Saturdays and Sundays 2–4.30. Telephone: (01756) 752800.

Gargrave. Although there is no commercial traffic on the canal these days it is busy with holiday craft in the summer.

Gargrave has long been important standing in a trans-Pennine pass made by the River Aire and utilised by road, canal and railway. The Normans built their castle lower down the river at Skipton, though a prehistoric fort overlooks the village from Steeling Hill. **Just as the road reaches Gargrave turn right, opposite the Victorian church, following a sign to Broughton, and cross the railway again.** A pleasant drive takes you back to the main road at Broughton. **Turn right when you meet the A59 towards Clitheroe and Colne and then, almost immediately, left on to an unsignposted road.** This leads to a fine bridge close to Broughton Hall (not open to the public). **Cross the bridge and follow the lane that passes an isolated church and then crosses a disused**

railway line. **Turn right at the T-junction at Elslack and then immediately left.** The lane climbs steadily. There is a grand view back and woodland to the left as the Pennine Way joins from the right.

At a T-junction at the top **E** **turn left.** There is a parking area here which is a good place for enjoying a wonderful view.

A little further on there is woodland to the left and moorland to the right. **Go straight over a crossroads to reach Carleton. Continue through the village and cross the River Aire and go under the bypass. Then follow the road into Skipton turning left on to the main road to follow signs to the town centre.** ■

The ramparts of Skipton Castle would daunt most attacking forces

MOUNT GRACE PRIORY, CAPTAIN COOK COUNTRY AND THE CLEVELAND HILLS

62 MILES – 3 HOURS
START AND FINISH AT MOUNT GRACE PRIORY

This is a long but satisfying drive which links scenery with history and architecture. The Cleveland Hills are the northernmost heights of the North Yorkshire Moors and overlook Teesside. Their deposits of ironstone were vital to the development of Middlesborough's industry. They rise above the village of Great Ayton, birthplace of Captain Cook, and the town of Guisborough, with its beautiful ruined priory. The tour returns through countryside which is particularly beautiful in late summer when the heather is in bloom.

Start the tour by visiting **Mount Grace Priory** which is situated about 5 miles north-east of Northallerton, just to the east of the A19.

Return down the driveway to the A19 and turn right across the dual carriageway to head towards Teesside. After just over 1 mile turn left off the dual carriageway to get on to the A172 towards Stokesley. The steep western escarpment of the North Yorkshire Moors can be seen to the right. **At Ingleby Arncliffe you can turn right to visit the church and walk in Arncliffe Wood.** The Cleveland Way crosses the moorland just above the woodland.

Continue along the A172 and, where the road divides at Stokesley, take the right-hand fork, the A173 **A** **to Kildale and Great Ayton.** Stokesley itself (reached by the B1366 to the left) is one of those places which has a stream running by its main street, and to reach the houses you have to cross over small bridges. It is very busy on Tuesday which is market-day.

The unmistakable shape of Roseberry Topping can now be

• PLACES OF INTEREST •

Mount Grace Priory
The remains of the priory are owned by the National Trust and administered by English Heritage. They are the best-preserved ruins of a monastery of the Carthusian Order to be seen in England. The monastery was founded in 1398 by Thomas de Holand, Earl of Surrey. The ruins illustrate the daily life of a medieval Carthusian priory. The monks did not live the communal life typical of other Orders – their lives were solitary, dedicated to work, study and worship. Food was delivered in such a way that the monks would not see the face of the person who brought it, the

dishes being pushed through an L-shaped recess. Each of the twenty-three monks in the community had his own cell with rooms which were used for various purposes. One such cell has been restored, and visitors can see the upstairs room where the brother did his weaving, his living quarters, and even his garden. At the time of the Dissolution of the monasteries there was a long waiting list of would-be monks hoping to come to Mount Grace.

Roseberry Topping
A fanciful legend links the distinctive hill, 1,051 feet

(320 m) high, with Osmotherley. The Queen of Northumbria dreamed that her baby son, Prince Oswy, would be drowned on a certain day. To thwart this she sent the prince and his attendant to the Topping on that day. Unfortunately, the attendant fell asleep and the toddler wandered off and fell into one of the springs which rise from the hillside. His mother died of grief when she learned what had happened, and she and her child were buried side-by-side at Osmotherley, which got its name because 'Os-by-his-mother-lay'.

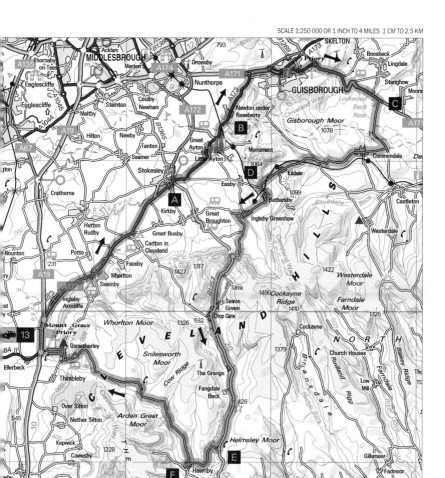

seen ahead. Old prints show that the Topping was once perfectly conical, but mining for ironstone lead to the collapse of the western face into a sheer cliff.

At Great Ayton turn right into the village. A pleasant stream, the infant River Leven, runs by the main street here. There is a car park at the top of the street where you may leave your car and explore the place where Captain Cook spent his early years. The church where he worshipped is on the other side of the main road.

From the car park continue along the road through the village to rejoin the A173, following the 'sailing ship' tour sign. About 1 mile out of Great Ayton, on the edge of

Mount Grace Priory – the best-preserved Carthusian monastery in Britain

the village of Newton under Roseberry, there is a car park and picnic site. You can undertake the climb up the mini-mountain, Roseberry Topping , from here. The climb to the summit at 1,051 feet (320 m) is very demanding. There is another parking space on the far side of Newton. At Pinchinthorpe you will find a picnic place from where you can take a walk in Guisborough Forest.

Turn right on to the A171 and then right again off the new bypass to visit Guisborough and its priory.

The main car park here is to the right of the main street and is close to the priory. However, bear in mind that market-days here are Thursdays and Saturdays when parking may be difficult.

Take the A171 out of town towards Whitby. The road soon climbs steeply to reach the top of the moors and there is a viewpoint, where the dual carriageway ends, at the summit of the bank. **After passing Lockwood Beck Reservoir on the right turn right** following the sign to **Castleton and Hutton-le-Hole.**

There is a superb view to the left after a cattle-grid, with another conical hill rising above rolling moorland, this is Freebrough Hill. A desolate stretch of moorland follows, where the snow-posts must be vital during winter. **At the first road junction at White Cross turn right to Commondale, Kildale and Stokesley.** There are soon views into Westerdale on the left.

The road drops down into Commondale very suddenly. Until the 1950s it had a busy brickworks fed by the railway. Now these have gone and the

---

• PLACES OF INTEREST •

Great Ayton
This is a lovely village in its own right, and would be a pleasant place to visit even without its association with Captain Cook whose parents moved here in 1736. The Captain Cook Museum is situated in the school he attended, though this was rebuilt subsequently. At least the school fared better than the cottage which was his father's retirement home – it was removed to Melbourne, Australia in 1934. A monument made of granite from Point Hicks, the first Australian land sighted by Cook, stands in its place. Another more prominent monument to Cook overlooks the village from Easby Moor.

The graves of the Cook family may be seen in the churchyard. The church itself, with its lovely unspoilt Georgian interior, is open most Sunday afternoons, but is otherwise locked.

Captain Cook's Schoolroom Museum, 101 High Street. Open April–July and September–October daily 2–4.30. August Mondays–Saturdays 10.30–12.30, 2–4.30. Telephone: (01642) 723911.

Guisborough
The priory, founded in 1119 by Norman de Brus (an ancestor of King Robert Bruce of Scotland), is correctly spelled Gisborough, like the hall on the outskirts of the

town. Because of fire and other disasters the priory had to be rebuilt three times – in spite of this it was an immensely wealthy Augustinian foundation.

Only the east end of the nave of the church survives, dating from 1286, but this is a masterpiece of Decorated architecture and indicates what a magnificent monastery this was before its dissolution in 1539.

The town grew up by the priory, and it must have caused distress when the monks were banished. The property was bought by Thomas Chaloner who used much of the fabric to build himself a magnificent residence nearby which has since been demolished. He promoted the mining of alum in the district in the early seventeenth century, a mineral important in the dyeing of fabrics, but this industry was short-lived and Guisborough had to wait for two hundred years before the discovery of ironstone brought new prosperity.

The church has some excellent medieval stained glass and a famous memorial to the Norman family who founded the priory, the Brus Cenotaph.

Gisborough Priory. Open April– September daily 10–1, 2–6. October– March Wednesdays– Sundays 10–1, 2–4. Telephone: (01287) 638301.

Ingleby Greenhow
There can be few churches that enjoy such a beautiful situation – St Andrew's stands by a rushing stream with a backcloth of woodland. Neither is the church itself a disappointment – it dates from the time of King Stephen, but was rebuilt in 1741. The capitals are decorated with faces of monsters and grotesque animals. Experts are divided over whether these were carved in medieval, Georgian, or even Victorian times. Pevsner suggests they may have

been done by a nineteenth-century rector, much to the indignation of the author of the church guide! The village stands at the foot of the Ingleby Incline: this railway dropped down from Blakey Howe, the wagons of iron ore being carefully lowered to the bottom and then taken off to Middlesbrough. Empty ones were hauled up to the top by a stationary steam engine. Today, a walk up the incline through the woods is a pleasant way to reach the crest of the moors.

land they occupied has been restored to make Commondale an attractive moorland village. It is popular with walkers who use the footpaths which lead either up to the moors or into the valley of the Esk.

Keep on the main road and cross over the railway line to reach Kildale. Here a tearoom can be found at Glebe Cottage on the road to the station. **Keep straight on towards Stokesley, passing under the railway line this time, until you come to a junction D. Turn left towards Battersby and Ingleby Greenhow. Continue over a level-crossing into Battersby. There is a shallow ford in the middle of the village.**

Battersby lies at the southern end of Kildale which penetrates the steep western escarpment of the Cleveland Hills and was used by the railway builders when they constructed the line to Whitby. However, today Battersby Junction sees unusual railway practice since trains from Middlesborough have to reverse here to complete their journey to Whitby.

At Ingleby Greenhow follow the turning left towards Great Broughton and Helmsley. Bear left again and cross a little bridge to reach another lane where you turn left to Chop Gate. You will enjoy the views of the hills ahead from this little road which snakes up

towards them. There are two picnic places in the forest – the second one on the right gives access to a fine viewpoint.

When the road meets the B1257 turn left towards Helmsley. Chop Gate is a useful place to park and explore the numerous footpaths which lead from this curiously-named village. The countryside to the south of the village is delightful. The pattern of fields on the hillside resembles a patchwork quilt.

After passing the church at Fangdale Beck you come to the isolated Sun Inn. Beyond this the road begins to twist and turn. Continue for about 2 miles and then look carefully for a turn on the right to Laskill E. Make this difficult right turn and go over the tiny bridge across the River Seph. This little road, giving lovely views, takes you to Hawnby, but it dips and then climbs very steeply before reaching the village.

Turn right F at Hawnby to

Osmotherley and Snilesworth. This is a pleasant moorland road with several laybys where you can enjoy a picnic or pause to enjoy the scenery. There is also an official picnic site at Hazel Head Wood when the road reaches the forest. Beyond the woods there are sections of the road which have steep gradients, but the delightful scenery is a compensation.

After a little bridge, just before Low Cote Farm, the road climbs up to empty moorland again. There is another car park on the top of these moors where the Cleveland Way joins the road from the south. Soon after this there is a tearoom at a farm shop. The road then drops down into Osmotherley, a pleasant village which once had an important market. **Bear right into Osmotherley at a T-junction, and then left by the church, heading for Northallerton. This road joins the A19 about 1 mile south of the driveway to Mount Grace.** ■

The unmistakable silhouette of Roseberry Topping

PICKERING AND DALBY FOREST

65 MILES – 3 HOURS
START AND FINISH AT PICKERING

The route begins by following the main road northwards parallel with Newton Dale (a detour is suggested on to Levisham Moor). It then visits Goathland and Beck Hole, two famous beauty spots. The most challenging part of the drive takes you through Littlebeck where the ford is occasionally impassable if there has been exceptional rainfall. However, you will usually cross it without difficulty and thus reach the coast at Robin Hood's Bay. The final part of the tour uses the toll road through Dalby Forest to take you back to Pickering. Note that some of the roads on this tour are very steep.

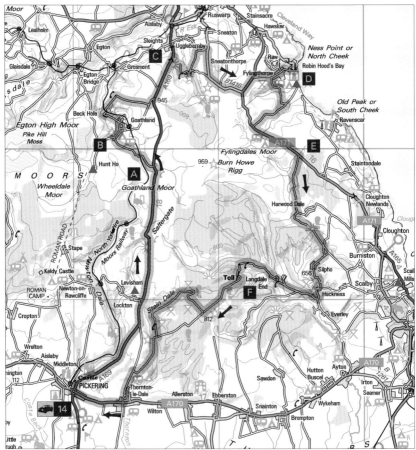

SCALE 1:250 000 OR 1 INCH TO 4 MILES 1 CM TO 2.5 KM

Leave Pickering on the A169 northwards towards Whitby. The scant remains of the castle are to the left as you leave the town. **Pass the Fox and Rabbit Inn and, 1 mile or so after this, look for a turn to the left to Lockton and Levisham. Take this road if you wish to make a detour over the moor and down into Newton Dale.** There are plenty of places to park and picnic before the road begins its tortuous descent to the station at Levisham.

Otherwise, continue northwards on the A169 to come to the Hole of Horcum. This is said to have been made when a giant named Wade scooped up a handful of earth to fling at his wife. It missed, and landed to the east to make Blakey Topping! There is a viewpoint car park on the right of the road and, from here, you can easily reach the footpaths leading down the slopes of the hole or walk along the crest of Newton Dale.

After the car park the road bends and drops to the Saltersgate Inn where it is said that the peat fire has been kept going for two hundred years. It was a popular inn with smugglers, and

At Goathland a path leads to the spectacular waterfall of Mallyan Spout

an explanation for the fire is that on one occasion a revenue man was killed and his body buried beneath the hearth, the fire being kept alight both to keep the corpse hidden and to prevent the murdered man's ghost from troubling the household. The pub also got its name from these smugglers – their main contraband being salt.

As the road continues across

the moor an enormous white concrete structure can be seen on the right. This is all that is left of the Fylingdales Early Warning Station – its famous golf balls have been dismantled. This part of the moor is particularly delightful in late summer when it is purple with heather. **After the road dips down to cross the Eller Beck take the turn on the left A to Goathland and Beck Hole.** There is a viewpoint car park on the left, just after the cattle-grid. The road drops down the valley to cross the beck again and then goes beneath the railway. There are wide views ahead after a caravan park with Goathland church tower clearly seen below.

At the T-junction B turn right towards Whitby. The footpath to Mallyan Spout, a spectacular waterfall, descends to the beck along a path which leaves the main road opposite the church. Goathland is a very spacious village with a long green so that its buildings are all set well back from the road.

Turn left near the end of Goathland on to a lane which goes to Beck Hole. The parish hall is to the left and, just after

---

• PLACES OF INTEREST •

Pickering
This market town is a delightfully light and airy place with many Georgian houses surrounding its church. It is overlooked by the castle. The latter began as a simple Norman motte-and-bailey structure (an earthen hill with a stockade on top, later replaced at Pickering by a stone keep). However, this was made more substantial in the thirteenth century to suit its new status as a royal hunting lodge. Most of the medieval kings visited Pickering to hunt in the extensive forest which then surrounded the town. However, military action brought about its ruin almost by accident. The Royalists stripped the lead from its roof to make shot for their

guns whilst they were defending Scarborough, and local landowners dismantled many of the walls for their stone.

Pickering's church has well-preserved medieval murals and strong ties with America, including a memorial to Robert King, a local man who surveyed Washington DC for George Washington in 1800.

Pickering is the southern terminus of the North Yorkshire Moors Railway and also has the excellent Beck Isle Museum.

North Yorkshire Moors Railway, Pickering Station. Steam locomotives take passengers through Newton Dale to Grosmont (though some trains are worked by classic diesel locomotives). Many believe this to be the finest

of all preserved lines in England, with the scenery being superb and the gradient providing an excellent challenge for the ancient engines.

Open Easter–October daily and 26 December–1 January. Telephone: (01751) 472508 or (01751) 473535.

Pickering Castle. Open April–September daily 10.00–6. October–March Wednesdays–Sundays 10–4. Telephone: (01751) 74989.

Beck Isle Museum of Rural Life, Bridge Street. Magnificent assortment of curious and commonplace items from the last two hundred years. Open daily end of March–31 October 10–4.30. Telephone: (01751) 473653.

Robin Hood's Bay

No one knows how the picturesque fishing village came by its name, which endows it with even more romance. Legend has it that on one of the many occasions when the famous outlaw was on the run he disguised himself as a fisherman here and so escaped arrest. The earliest record of the name is in 1538.

Much of the charm of the village is in the way that the houses are huddled about its steep streets (no cars are allowed). Many of them are only accessible by steps, and the observant will notice the first-floor 'coffin windows' in many of them which also served to bring furniture into and out of the dwelling. None of the buildings on the seaward side of the village are older than 1780 when a great storm swept away much of the main street. At one time more than one hundred fishing boats sailed from here. It was a place notorious for contraband. There are lovely clifftop walks in both directions as well as a fascinating geological trail.

Dalby Forest

The 8-mile drive through Dalby Forest begins at Bickley Gate, where you pay your toll. You may wish to visit the Forest Garden to be introduced to the main trees grown in the forests of Britain. Two forest walks begin from the car park here. The Deepdale Habitat Trail is the shorter one and takes you through land specially preserved to benefit wildlife within the forest. Staindale is one of the most popular parts of the forest. It has a lake where children can feed the wildfowl. There is a lakeside path for wheelchair visitors. Three walks start from here, the longest taking you to the Crossliff viewpoint which can also be reached by car. Finally, you come to Dalby village where there is a visitor centre and the starting point for more walks, including a streamside ramble beside Dalby Beck. You can camp in the forest in a caravan or under canvas, and there are excellent facilities for cycling, orienteering, and bird- and bat-watching.

Low Dalby Visitor Centre.
Open Easter–October daily 11–5.
Telephone: Forest District Office
(01751) 72771.

---

this, a footpath crosses descending straight down to the bottom of the valley. This path follows the course of the Goathland Incline, where many years ago trains were hauled up from the bottom of the valley by a steam-engine located at the top. There was a terrible accident in 1864 when the rope broke and the train crashed to the bottom.

Bear left at the next road junction to Beck Hole where the road descends and then climbs at gradients of 1-in-4. Beck Hole is one of the most popular beauty spots in North Yorkshire, and there is parking on the right before the steep descent into the village. There are spectacular views when the climb up from the village eases and you are able to see through the trees to the left. Soon the road is on open moorland again. **At the junction at the top of the hill turn left to Whitby and, after a short distance, join with the A169.**

Whitby is soon seen ahead, with its church and ruined abbey on the clifftop. **At Blue Bank the road descends a gradient of 1-in-5. Be particularly careful since, halfway down the hill, you need to make a very sharp turn to the right to Littlebeck . This lane descends at an even steeper angle (1-in-3). The fine views are a distraction as the road winds down – use first gear here!

After crossing a stream the climb up the other side is equally steep. Just when you think the worst of the gradients are over the road descends, again very steeply, to a ford. Wainwright's Coast to Coast route also crosses the Little Beck here, and there is a car park just after the ford.

When the road divides keep on the major road to the left towards Robin Hood's Bay. The road to the right is the shorter route, but is for local traffic only. The lane climbs steeply and then passes through a farmyard with buildings of warm-coloured stone. **Keep straight on, enjoying even better views to reach the B1416. Turn right towards Scarborough.** The 1-in-7 ascent that follows seems negligible after those climbed previously! At the end of a straight length of road, which goes on for about

The houses perched on the clifftop are an ever-popular subject for photographers at Robin Hood's Bay

1½ miles, the B1416 bends sharply to the left. The roads to the right lead to beauty spots in Sneaton Forest. Bear right to reach Falling Foss. This is a 30-foot (9 m) waterfall. The other road goes past a caravan site to a picnic site by May Beck. There are waymarked walks here as well as another waterfall.

Otherwise, when the B1416 meets the A171 turn left towards Whitby and Robin Hood's Bay. After just under 1 mile turn right to Robin Hood's Bay and Fylingthorpe. Now there are extensive views over the coast, with the red roofs of the houses at Robin Hood's Bay on the cliff ahead. There is a picnic place on the moor here, before the road begins to drop down into Fylingthorpe.There is a café and art gallery on the left before the church. **At the T-junction turn right towards Robin Hood's Bay car park** **.** Even if you do not take the steep walk down to the bay it is worth going this far just to see the view of the coastline.

Retrace your route through Fylingthorpe. As you climb up the hill after the village take the lane on the left to Fyling Hall (this turn comes before the start of the steepest part of the climb). The lane twists through park gates and then passes Fyling Hall School (an old manor house). It becomes very narrow as it goes behind the servants' quarters and stables, being hardly wider than an alley-way. Beyond this the lane is delightful, dropping down into woods and then climbing out of them again. There are places here where you can pause to enjoy the coastal view, with footpaths going towards the cliffs. **The lane eventually meets a major road going to the delightfully-named Boggle Hole.** This is a favourite haunt for fossil hunters. **If you do not wish to visit the shore here turn right towards Scarborough, climb back**

Howden Hill, seen shortly before the start of the Forest Drive

to the A171 and turn left on to this towards Scarborough.

Pass the Flask Inn on the right and continue for a short distance into the forest. Look for a turn E **to the right soon after entering the forest signposted to Harwood Dale.** As you turn watch out for oncoming traffic which often speed on this stretch of road. There are plenty of picnic places in the forest and, as you emerge from it, Rosalie's Tearoom is to the right.

Follow the main road heading for Silpho and Hackness when the road to Harwood Dale leaves to the left. The road climbs up to the picnic place and viewpoint at Reasty Bank. **Bear right at a crossroads and then turn right at a T-junction into Silpho.** There is another viewpoint and picnic place soon after this village as the road begins to drop into a wooded valley. The descent passes through trees crowding on to the road and twists through a series of hairpin bends to reach Hackness.

Turn right at the main road towards Forge Valley. Keep on the main road at the next junction towards the Dalby Forest Drive, passing Hackness Grange Hotel. Howden Hill is the conical hill ahead as the road descends to cross the River Derwent at

Langdale End. It is an outlier of the main massif, its soft clay being protected by a cap of hard sandstone which gives it its shape.

When you come to a T-junction turn left again to Dalby Forest Drive and Bickley. Soon afterwards the toll-road starts F and, throughout its length, there are parking places, walks, picnic sites and adventure playgrounds. **Near the start of the drive a signpost points to the Crosscliff viewpoint which is worth visiting for a fine panorama north-westwards. Return to the main drive after this short detour to pass an entrance to Jingleby Farm.** The farm has a tea garden. You will pass a picturesque lake before coming to Low Dalby where there is an interpretation centre. This area is part of the largest upland heath forest in England. The oldest trees were planted in 1924, and by the year 2010 there will be sustainable production of 120,000 tons of timber annually.

When you pass out of the forest turn left at a main road to Thornton-le-Dale. This is another celebrated beauty spot with a stream running through the centre of the village. You will find places for refreshment and gift shops here.

Turn right at the centre of the village to return to Pickering on the A170. ■

YORK, KIRKHAM PRIORY AND CASTLE HOWARD

48 MILES - 2 HOURS
START AND FINISH AT YORK

This tour leaves York and follows the River Derwent northwards to visit beautiful Kirkham Priory. It then passes through Malton, a busy market town full of character, reflecting the best aspects of Yorkshire's way of living. The highlight of the drive must be Castle Howard – easily the most magnificent of the country's historic houses.

Take the A1079 out of York towards Hull and the East Coast. At the roundabout, which crosses the bypass, keep in the left-hand lane to take the A166 towards Bridlington. The Yorkshire Museum of Farming is on the left at Murton. Set in eight acres of tranquil countryside there are many farm animals to admire – cattle, sheep, pigs, horses and poultry. There are also several reconstructions including James Herriot's surgery and Houlgate, a village of the Dark Ages.

The landscape of the Vale of York is flat and rather featureless at this point, with the Wolds rising up ahead in the distance. **Ignore the first turning to Buttercrambe to the left. As you come into Stamford Bridge turn left Ⓐ before traffic lights on to another lane signposted to Buttercrambe.** Stamford Bridge was the scene of a battle in 1066 which altered the course of history. King Harold's army was on the south coast awaiting the invasion threatened by William of Normandy when he learned

that his brother had joined with a Danish army to claim the throne. Harold hurried to the north and his troops managed to win a notable victory here. However, the army was depleted by the battle and then had to undertake another march southwards to meet the Normans at Hastings. How they would have fared had they been fresh and strong is one of those enigmas which occupy military historians.

Another fateful encounter took place on this same battlefield in 1453 – the first battle of the Wars of the Roses.

After ¹/₂ mile turn right at the T-junction and continue to Buttercrambe. The entrance to Aldby Park, a fine brick mansion, is to the left. **Cross two narrow bridges which take the road over the River Derwent and keep on the main road heading for Leavening and Malton.** Those with an interest in bloodstock will like to know that in 1704 the Darley Arabian was brought here from Aleppo. His owner, James Darley, lived at the Mill House by the bridge (the house that previously stood there has been replaced by the present Georgian building).

Go straight over a crossroads at the top of a hill. Three miles after this the road reaches another hilltop crossroads. Just beyond this take the turn on the left signposted to Westow and Kirkham Priory. This road leads to Westow, a village of red-roofed cottages with a fine eighteenth-century manor house to the right. **Immediately after the Blacksmith's Arms turn left to Kirkham and York.** The road follows the beautifully-wooded Derwent valley. There is another handsome manor house to the

• PLACES OF INTEREST •

York
There are so many places to visit in this city that it is impossible to cover everything here! A section has been devoted to York in the introduction (page 13). For further information on specific places of interest contact the Tourist Information Centre at De Grey Rooms, Exhibition Square. Telephone: (01904) 621756.

Kirkham Priory
The finest feature of this priory is its thirteenth-century gatehouse notable for its heraldry and

sculpture, which includes St George and the Dragon and David and Goliath. This is a splendid example of Decorated architecture.

The abbey was founded for the Augustinian order by Walter l'Espée c. 1125. He also founded Rievaulx for the Cistercians and another monastery in Bedfordshire. However, at Kirkham, Walter's work is masked by a great spree of building which took place a little later, and it is mainly this which survives.

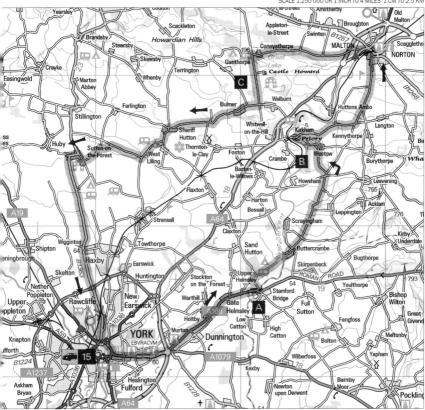

right as you drop down to the ruined Kirkham Priory **B**.

Retrace your route up the hill and turn left just before the pub to Firby, Langton and Malton. Soon the road is high up on the wolds and there are striking views. **Bear left twice, once when you meet a road from Westow and again to join the main road to Malton. Continue into the neighbouring township of Norton, where you cross the railway line and the river to enter Malton. Turn left at the town centre traffic lights on to the A64 (York road). Just after the war memorial on the right, branch right to Coneysthorpe, Terrington and Castle Howard.**

The road leads to views of a tidy countryside of cornfields and trees. As the route approaches the Castle Howard estate patches of woodland become more numerous – this

is a very attractive landscape. Coneysthorpe is an estate village; the main street is to the right and the Georgian church is set between lines of cottages which, in the other direction, lead the eye straight to Castle Howard standing majestically in the distance. **Turn left at the crossroads which follows and pass through**

portals. Another view of the great mansion on the far side of the lake can now be seen. There are parking places on the right here. An avenue of lime trees leads to the obelisk **C** which was erected in 1714 and commemorates the building of the house. The entrance to the house is to the left.

The River Derwent at Kirkham Priory

The romantic outline of Castle Howard, seen from the road

• PLACES OF INTEREST •

Malton
The town's history began in Roman times when, in the latter half of the first century, they built a fort just below the present bridge to protect the river crossing. A settlement grew up around this and the Normans, arriving here about a thousand years later, used the Roman defences as the foundation for a new stronghold which lasted until the seventeenth century. Old Malton is to the north-east of the main town and was centred on the Priory founded here c.1150. Parts of this were incorporated into St Mary's Church. Malton's heyday seems to have been in Georgian times when it was a staging-point on the road to Scarborough as well as for north-south routes. Many of its buildings date from this era.

Dickens was a friend of Charles Smithson, a solicitor in the town, and visited him at Malton. He is supposed to have described Smithson's office in *A Christmas Carol* as the place where Scrooge tormented poor Bob Cratchit. This gives Malton the excuse to put on an enjoyable Dickensian festival just before Christmas each year. Today, Malton continues as a busy market town and tourist centre (it makes a good base for

exploring the Moors, Wolds, York and the coast). It is also a centre for horseracing with many stables based nearby.

Malton Museum, Town Hall, Market Place. Collection of artefacts illustrating the history of Malton, from c. 8000 BC to the medieval era, with special emphasis on Roman times.

Open Easter–31 October Mondays–Saturdays 10–4. Sundays 2–4. Telephone: (01653) 695136 or 692610.

Eden Camp Modern History Theme Museum, Old Malton. Situated off the A169 just to the north of the town. The exhibits depict the civilian way of life during the Second World War, at which time a thousand prisoners-of-war were held here.

Open 14 February– 23 December daily 10–5 (last admission 4). Telephone: (01653) 697777.

Castle Howard
Evelyn Waugh had Castle Howard in mind when he wrote *Brideshead Revisited*, so it was entirely appropriate to use it as the setting when the story was filmed. This brought new visitors to the house, which it deserves, for it is in the first division of grand

English palaces alongside Blenheim and Chatsworth. It was built for the Howard family by Sir John Vanbrugh in the early 1700s. It is puzzling why Vanbrugh was chosen as architect – he had no other grand works to his credit at the time and was known only as a successful playwright (his first career had been as a captain of marines). However, he set to work with zest and some cunning – he appointed Nicholas Hawksmoor, Wren's clerk of works at St Paul's, to a similar post at Castle Howard. There is an enduring dispute about which architect was responsible for the mansion and the various features which surround it. It is enough to say here that it is a masterpiece of architecture whose interior matches the exterior in sumptuousness. Visitors will see statues brought from Italy and Greece, Chippendale and Sheraton furniture, and paintings by artists like Gainsborough and Rubens. There is an exhibition of costumes. Visitors can also roam through the gardens (famous for their roses) and many of the thousand acres of parkland.

Open Easter–October daily. Grounds from 10, house from 11.00–4.30. Telephone: (01653) 648333.

Keep straight on, if you are not intending to visit the house, through another grand entrance surmounted by a pyramid. The drive can be seen ahead for another mile or so pursuing its switchback course, but halfway along this road there is another gateway. This one is the Carrmire Gate, framed by castellated walls with bastion towers. **Shortly after this, turn right at the crossroads to Bulmer, Terrington and Sheriff Hutton.** There are views over the hedges to rolling fields dotted with trees. Bulmer has a fine Norman church on the left and the usual broad street. There is a tearoom at the post office about halfway along.

The road goes steeply down to cross a beck, and a little later you will see the ruins of Sherriff Hutton Castle on the skyline ahead. **At a crossroads on the edge of the village turn left to Strensall and York and pass the Highwayman pub.** Both the church and the castle are to the left of the road, though the latter is on private property. The church is unusually dedicated to St Helen and the Holy Cross. Richard III's son Edward, who died aged eleven in 1484, is buried in the church and his alabaster effigy may be seen there.

The entrance to Sheriff Hutton Park is to the left as you leave the village and the road swings to the right towards Strensall and York. The present house dates from

Sherriff Hutton Castle

The remains of the castle are on the south side of the village and may be reached by a footpath. Remarkably, it was originally the size and shape of Bolton Castle, with four towers 100 feet (30.5 m) high. It was built by John, Lord Neville of Raby, in 1382 and, though little survives, it is still worth visiting. It has details such as fireplaces and garderobes (lavatories) still intact.

Furthermore, the place is steeped in history – it has connections with Richard III who held his young nephew Edward, Earl of Warwick, prisoner here. He was allowed to walk as far as an oak tree in the grounds of Sherriff Hutton Park. The pasture in which that oak stood is still known as

Warwick Field. Elizabeth of York was also held prisoner here by Richard – he hoped that she would agree to marry him and thus make his claim to the throne more legitimate, but she repulsed his efforts.

In 1535 Leland called the castle princely but, less than one hundred years later, it was in decay, with stone being taken from its walls by local landowners.

1619 and was built in brick by Sir Arthur Ingram, the same material used for his other residence, Temple Newsam House at Leeds. The park and garden (which is also Jacobean) are open on week days, but the hall is presently occupied by an acting school and theatre company.

After another mile take the turn to the right to Sutton-on-the-Forest. The landscape is now richly agricultural. **After a straight stretch of road take a turn to the left to Sutton.** The road goes below big power lines. **At a T-junction turn left again for Sutton and York.**

At the next unsignposted T-junction turn right and then, after 1/2 mile, left on to the B1363 to go down Sutton's long main street. The entrance to Sutton Park is halfway along this on the left, just before the church. You get a good view of the eighteenth-century house through a gateway opposite the church. The garden, with its colourful terraces, is open daily.

The village gets its name from the Forest of Galtres which was a wild and lawless place in medieval times. Packs of wolves and bands of outlaws roamed the dense woodland which was largely of oak trees. However, by the seventeenth century most of its great trees had been felled and fields and meadows had replaced the forest. Laurence Sterne was vicar of Sutton from 1738 until his death, though from 1760 he lived at Coxwold where he wrote *Tristram Shandy*.

At the end of the street the B1363 bears left. Follow this to pass through Wigginton, cross the ring road, and thus reach York. ■

The beautiful formal gardens at Sutton Park

WHITBY, STAITHES, DANBY AND ESK DALE

47 MILES – 2¹⁄₂ HOURS
START AND FINISH AT WHITBY

This route embraces a fine stretch of coastline, covers equally exhilarating moorland, and then follows beautiful Esk Dale, the only dale in the North Yorkshire Moors to follow a west-east course. There are steep gradients on this route, but in compensation it does take you along largely unfrequented and beautiful byways. There is also a ford which may be impassable after heavy rain – an attractive diversion is suggested to avoid this if necessary.

Head out of Whitby on the A174 towards Saltburn, passing a golf course on the right. Continue through Sandsend. The village takes its name from being at the western end of Whitby Sands – there are

cliffs all the way to Saltburn from here. It is a pleasant little fishing village with roadside parking. The road drops down to cross the beck and from the bridge there is a good view of the red-roofed fishermen's cottages.

There can be few more beautiful fishing villages than Staithes

It then climbs up Lythe Bank and a road to the right goes to Kettleness, famous for being the headland where Count Dracula's ship went aground.

At Ellerby turn right off the main road to visit Runswick Bay. From here there are wonderful views of the coastline. Fishing boats drawn up above the tide-line provide a colourful foreground for the old houses of the village.

Return to the A174 by taking the road to Hinderwell. Continue along the coast road for another 2 miles before turning right to visit Staithes. Photographs on millions of calendars have made Staithes a world-famous beauty spot, its cottages clinging to cliffs overlooking a snug harbour. Ladies in the village occasionally wear traditional white bonnets. The village also has associations with Captain Cook who was apprenticed to a draper with a shop near the harbour. The car park is at the top of the village and the walk down the hill is quite steep. There is no parking at the bottom.

Return once more to the coast road and continue past the Boulby potash mine. This has the deepest shaft in Britain

Whitby

The town has had an influence on the maritime history of England quite disproportionate with its size. Ships sailing from Whitby, most of them having been built there, have journeyed to all corners of the world – Captain Cook, who learned his seamanship here, used four Whitby-built ships for his voyages to the Pacific. The country has always been quick to call up the Whitby fleet and crews in times of emergency. Many were employed in the east-coast trade in coal and alum, the latter being particularly important to the growth of the town in the seventeenth century. Other boats sailed far away in search of whales, while many more were engaged in the traditional industry of fishing which survives to this day. Whitby kippers are particularly celebrated.

Any visitor to the town will want to visit the abbey which stands on the clifftop overlooking the harbour. This grew from a small settlement established by St Hilda in 657 where Caedmon,

'the father of English poetry', was cowherd. In 664 the monastery was the venue for the Synod of Whitby which reconciled the Celtic church with that of Rome. St Hilda's Abbey was later destroyed by Vikings and the traces of the Norman one which succeeded it have also disappeared. The dramatic ruins seen today are those of the abbey built between the thirteenth and fifteenth centuries. They have survived the onslaught of the weather remarkably well since the Dissolution – the great tower above the Crossing only collapsed in 1830.

St Mary's Church also stands on the clifftop at the top of the 199 steps which wind up from the harbour. It is well worth the effort, being a delightful hotchpotch of medieval mixed with Georgian.

Whitby Abbey. Open April–September daily 10–6. October–March daily 10–4. Telephone: (01947) 603568.

Whitby Museum, Pannett Park. A wide-ranging exhibition

illustrating the town's history, including Captain Cook items.

Open May–September Mondays– Fridays 9.30–5.30, Sundays 2–4. October–April Mondays and Tuesdays 10.30–1, Wednesdays– Saturdays 10.30–4, Sundays 2–4. Closed at Christmas. Telephone: (01947) 602908.

Captain Cook Memorial Museum, Grape Lane. This was the house of John Walker to whom Captain Cook was apprenticed when he first went to sea. Cook lodged here and there are two rooms furnished as it was in his day. There are also models, manuscripts and pictures.

Open March and November weekends 11–3. April–October daily 9.45–4.30. Telephone: (01947) 601900.

Sutcliffe Gallery, 1 Flowergate. Display devoted to Frank Meadow Sutcliffe's nineteenth-century photographs. Open all year except Christmas and New Year, Mondays–Saturdays 9–5, Easter– Christmas Sundays 1–5. Telephone: (01947) 602239.

SCALE 1:250 000 OR 1 INCH TO 4 MILES 1 CM TO 2.5 KM

Grosmont Station on the North Yorkshire Moors Railway

some 3,750 feet (1,143 m) deep. **Turn left as you come into the village of Easington. The road goes past the splendid Grinkle Park Hotel to reach the A171 after about 5 miles. Turn right here and then take the first turn left to Danby, Castleton and Hutton-le-Hole.** This is a pleasant moorland road giving extensive views. **After about 1 mile, just before the top of the hill, turn left at a well-disguised junction.**

The lane leads to a wonderful viewpoint on Danby Beacon which gives views round 360 degrees. Scaling Dam Reservoir can be seen to the north with the coastline beyond. **Descend the hill from the beacon and take the little lane on the left.** There are even better views of Eskdale and Danby from here. This is a good place for a picnic. **Turn right when this lane meets another road and descend into Danby. Take the first turn on the left to the car park at the Moors Centre.** This is reached before you get to the village itself.

The centre, located in Danby Lodge, is the headquarters of the North Yorkshire Moors National Park, and you can learn much about the park from the film shows and exhibitions here. The lodge is surrounded by thirteen acres of fields, woodland and gardens and,

as well as waymarked walks, play and picnic areas, there is also an orienteering course. Refreshments are available.

Turn right out of the car park and left at the T-junction on to a road which climbs to Danby village and Castleton. There is a fine view before Danby village where a good choice of refreshments is available.

At the crossroads, by the Duke of Wellington pub in the village centre, turn left to cross the railway line and the river. The byway to the left goes to Duck Bridge, a medieval pack-horse bridge built by a man of that name. **Keep on to turn left just before the fire station to pass the Fox and Hounds Inn on the left. Continue along this road to Danby Castle .**

The castle was the home of

Catherine Parr, the surviving wife of Henry VIII. It is of much the same date as Bolton Castle (late fourteenth century) and, remarkably, was not very much smaller. The ruin standing today looks like the remains of a simple border tower joined with a much later farmhouse, but it was originally a mighty stronghold built by the Latimer family. An interesting survival of its old importance is the annual Leet Jury held here to adjudicate on the rents and disputes over the common grazing.

The road continues to follow the contours of the hillside high above the dale, striking southwards. **After passing behind Crossley Side Farm keep on the major road, bearing left, when another road climbs steeply off to the right.**

The road now heads down to cross Little Fryup (pronounced 'Freep') Beck. The hill to the left, fringed with Scots pines, is Fairy Cross Plain where fairies are reputed to make butter at night. Standing between the two branches of the Fryup Dale it is a magnificent viewpoint. A bridleway climbs up it just after Stonebeck Gate Farm, about 1/2 mile from the last junction.

Turn sharply left towards Glaisdale and Lealholm when a road goes to the right to Fryupdalehead. Go through the hamlet of Low Garth. This

Whitby harbour with the church and abbey beyond

is just a handful of houses and a village hall. After Furnace Farm, a name recalling the iron-smelting industry, a road from Houlsyke joins from the left and you will pass several other minor roads as the route follows the southern side of Esk Dale. **Keep ahead over a crossroads where the turn to the right goes to Rosedale. Pass Wind Hill Farm on the left to come to a major road. Turn right towards Glaisdale which is 1 mile from here.**

Follow the main road through the village. Pass the church to the right and descend to the station. There is a tearoom here opposite Beggar's Bridge. Climb Limber Hill where there is a gradient of 1-in-3. There are fine views at the top back to Glaisdale. **Turn right C when the road divides, following the sign to Egton Bridge and Goathland.** The road now descends steeply to go beneath the railway and runs close to the river. **At Egton Bridge turn right at the T-junction on to the road to Goathland and Pickering and cross the river over the new bridge.** Egton Bridge has a large Catholic church which reflects the strong hold that the religion has in this district. One of the last martyrs to die for the Old Faith was Father Nicholas Postgate who was executed in York in 1679 for baptising a child here. He

---

• PLACES OF INTEREST •

Glaisdale

The village is a good starting point for walks, many of them using the tracks made by iron-ore miners in the nineteenth century. The path through East Arncliffe Wood to Egton Bridge is particularly enjoyable.

The lovely Beggar's Bridge at Glaisdale was built in 1619 by Tom Ferris. When he was a penniless youth living in Glaisdale he had courted a girl from Egton. The courtship was not easy since he had difficulty in seeing her – at that time there was no bridge across the Esk at Glaisdale and, in any case, her father considered Tom to be a worthless beggar. The broken-hearted young man took himself off to sea and fought against the Armada. Subsequently he became very wealthy, being made Lord Mayor of Hull and Master of Trinity House. However, he never forgot his roots or his prospective father-in-law's judgement of his character. He returned to have the bridge built so that, he said, other couples might find their courting easier. Some versions of the tale say that he returned and married his early sweetheart, but most deny us this happy ending.

was eighty-two years old and became known as the Martyr of the Moors. The Postgate pub in the village is named after him.

Pass the Horseshoe Hotel and bear left towards Goathland when the road signposted to Rosedale leaves to the right. The lane winds up beneath overhanging trees. **Near the top the main road bears left, still going towards Goathland. However, 1/4 mile after this, leave the Goathland road by bearing left towards the Esk valley.**

The road bears a warning: 'Deep ford 1/2 mile ahead frequently impassable' but, unless there has been very heavy rain in the previous twenty-four hours, the crossing should not prove difficult – there are indicator posts at the ford to show the depth of the water.

If there has been recent heavy rain, or you do not wish to cross this ford, it would be best to make for Goathland and then head for Whitby on the A169.

The road down to the ford **D** is gated after the railway bridge. **After crossing the River Esk turn right on to the main road into Grosmont.** Cross a bridge and look right to see a fine railway bridge also

spanning the river – the Murk Esk, a tributary which flows from Mallyan Spout. There is a car park to the left. The road then goes under the railway line and over the level-crossing by Grosmont station – a terminus of the North Yorkshire Railway connecting with trains to Whitby and Middlesborough.

Follow the road up through the village, bearing left at two junctions towards Sleights. Soon the houses of the village appear ahead and the road meets the A169. Sleights has many fine houses built by the ship-owners and merchants of Whitby – they preferred to live a little distance from the seaport which brought them their wealth.

Turn left on to the A169 towards Whitby and cross the railway and the River Esk. This is now a considerable stream tamed by weirs. It is a popular place with fly fishermen hoping to catch salmon or trout. **Turn right immediately after the river-bridge on to the B1410 which follows the river to Ruswarp.** This stretch of river is very beautiful and there are boats to hire and riverside cafés. **At Ruswarp turn left on to the B1416 and then right along the A171 to return to Whitby.** ∎

77

KIRKBYMOORSIDE, CASTLETON AND ROSEDALE

39 MILES – 2 HOURS
START AND FINISH AT KIRKBYMOORSIDE

Good visibility is required to get maximum enjoyment from this tour which takes you through some of the finest scenery of the North Yorkshire Moors. You will see Hutton-le-Hole, a village famous for its beauty and for the Ryedale Folk Museum. The route then follows Blakey Ridge to Castleton and, after this, you may like to visit the Moors Centre at Danby if you have not done so previously. The return crosses Danby and Rosedale moors and takes you to Lastingham. Do not miss the opportunity to see the Norman crypt of Lastingham's parish church.

Head eastwards out of Kirkbymoorside on the A170 (Pickering road). After 1 mile take the turning left signposted to Hutton-le-Hole and Castleton. After climbing steadily through woodland there are a few picnic places on Hutton Common on the left. Hutton-le-Hole **A** is the archetypal moorland village with sheep grazing on a wide green bisected by a sparkling stream. The Ryedale Folk Museum is to the right and the car park 100 yards (91 m) up the Lastingham road, also on the right, at the end of the village. **Keep straight on through Hutton-le-Hole and climb steadily to Blakey Ridge on top of the moors.** There are grand views westwards over Farndale to Rudland Rigg and Bransdale Moor from the crest of the ridge, especially if you stop the car and walk for a couple of hundred yards across the heather. If you are lucky you will disturb a grouse and be startled by its quick, noisy flight. There is a choice of picnic places here, and the moorland is particularly glorious when the heather is out in the late summer.

Continue past the Lion Inn B. This is one of the highest pubs in the county at about 1,300 feet (396 m). A sheep fair is held here in autumn.

Two miles further on you will pass the medieval moorland cross known as Young Ralph, the symbol of the National Park. Old Ralph is a smaller cross located about 200 yards (183 m) across the heather. There is one tradition that coins should be left on top of the cross for poor wayfarers who may pass them. Unfortunately, this led to the cross being broken into three pieces in the 1960s when someone climbed it for this bounty. It is also said that, should three kings ever meet here, the

• PLACES OF INTEREST •

Kirkbymoorside
Kirkbymoorside has been an important market town since the Middle Ages and, on market days (Wednesdays), the stalls occupy the wide main street. The old inns which line the street testify to the town's importance in the days of the stagecoach. Nothing remains of the Norman castle which stood to the north of the town, apart from the shape of its moat. The church has lost all of its Norman work though much remains from medieval times.

Kirkbymoorside was the death-place of George Villiers, second Duke of Buckingham, the debauched favourite of Charles II. He died in 1687, either from a fall from his horse or from a chill caught when riding. It is said that he died in the worst room of the worst inn. His intestines were buried in Helmsley and the rest of his body in Westminster Abbey.

Ryedale Folk Museum, Hutton-le-Hole.
A small doorway leads into a large area where thirteen buildings have been reconstructed to give an insight into how people lived and worked in neighbouring villages in the past. There is a medieval garth cottage, an Elizabethan manor house, and a number of old shops. Craftsmen demonstrate traditional skills and there are frequent special events like 'Try-it-yourself Days'.
Open Easter –October daily 10–5.30. Telephone: (01751) 417367.

world will end. Furthermore, if the heather and bog surrounding the crosses are covered by snow three times before Christmas the rest of the winter will be mild. The presence of these medieval crosses at this high, lonely crossroads at Rosedale Head shows the importance and antiquity of the ways which meet here – a road to Rosedale goes off to the right almost opposite the cross. From here, on a clear day, you can see the coast in one direction and, if you are very keen-eyed, York Minster in the other.

At the Cross a road leaves to the left to Westerdale. **Keep on the main road to Castleton.** The view ahead opens up, and you begin to see the coastline ahead beyond the unmistakable chimney of Boulby mine. A little further and you will see Castleton as well, its buildings straggling along the side of Esk Dale.

Castleton takes its name from the Norman castle erected here by Robert de Brus c.1160. Robert was ancestor of the Scottish king who we know better as Robert the Bruce. It was unpretentious, a simple stone keep on a steep mound without bailey walls. The remains of it can be seen to the right of the Guisborough road, about 300 yards (274 m) beyond Castleton's main street. The village is quiet these days, especially in the winter, and it is hard to imagine it bustling with industry and commerce. Yet, a hundred years ago it had a busy woollen mill and a market serving the farmers working the rich land of the Esk valley.

Go straight through Castleton, descending all the time, to a small bridge. Turn right C after this on to the road signposted to Ainthorpe and Fryup. (If you wish to visit the Moors Centre at Danby continue staight on here.) Climb a hill and pass a war memorial on the slope to the right.

Go past a turn to Botton

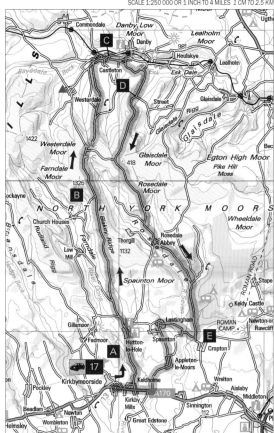

Hutton-le-Hole

Castleton Rigg from Ainthorpe – inviting footpaths start from here

on the right by a school to come to the fire station. Just beyond this make an acute turn right on to the road to Fryup, passing the Fox and Hounds inn. There is a lovely view just beyond the pub over the dale to the right. Many footpaths thread their way on to Danby Rigg from points near Rowantree Farm. As you approach Danby Castle there are good views to the left of Danby village. The remains of the castle, constructed of square blocks of stone, are incorporated into farm buildings. Similar stone can be seen utilised in other buildings in this locality. Obviously their source was this stronghold which was once of considerable size. In its heyday it must have been magnificent in this setting, though even these fragments remain very picturesque. The castle was once the home of Catherine Parr, the sixth and last wife of Henry VIII.

Cross a cattle-grid and pass Crossley Side Farm and then, when the road forks just after this, bear right D and climb steeply to the top of the ridge. There are wonderful views to the left and a couple of picnic places on the way up in old quarries.

• *PLACES OF INTEREST* •

Rosedale
It is hard to imagine that Rosedale was once the site of a mining boom-town, alive with noise and bustle. A railway line from Rosedale followed the top of the moors, crossing the Hutton-le-Hole to Castleton road just south of the Lion Inn, and then followed the contours around the head of Farndale to reach the top of the incline above Ingleby Greenhow. The ore was roasted before being dispatched on the railway, and the remains of the calcinating kilns can still be visited.

In 1851 the population of Rosedale was 558, but within twenty years this had risen to a peak of 2,839. The General Strike of 1926 saw the demise of the mines, and the engines from the railway were lowered down the Ingleby incline in 1929.

Today the valley has regained its tranquillity, and the most prominent monument to the industry, the 100-foot- (30.5 m) high chimney which stood at the top of Chimney Bank on the road to Hutton-le-Hole and gave it its name, has been demolished.

Lastingham Church
St Cedd founded a monastery here in 654. He and many of his community were struck down with plague ten years later. Cedd was succeeded as abbot by his younger brother St Chad, and the abbey flourished until it was destroyed by the Danes in the ninth century.

In 1078 Stephen, Abbot of Whitby, persuaded William I to restore Lastingham, and he set to work on the abbey, building the magnificent crypt as a shrine to St Cedd. However, in about 1086 Stephen and his monks left abruptly to set up a new monastery in York leaving only the crypt and the apse of the church complete.

Amazingly, the crypt has survived unaltered over the succeeding centuries. It is a self-contained church in its own right and its Norman style is massively impressive. The church, enlarged as a parish church in medieval times, suffered remarkably little from a restoration in 1878.

The road is soon on top of Danby High Moor. It is narrow and there are not many passing places. Generally you can see a long way ahead if visibility is good. A tumulus to the right of the road has the name of Wolf Pit, a reminder that wolves were still to be found here in medieval times. On a good day Roseberry Topping can be seen clearly to the right from here. Again, to enjoy these views properly you must leave the car.

At a T-junction turn left to Rosedale. The road continues on open moorland before making a roller-coaster descent to Rosedale Abbey. The abbey was, in fact, a Cistercian nunnery founded in the twelfth century, but there are scant remains of it, and today the small village lives largely from tourism.

Leave the village on the Pickering road passing the Coach House Pub on the left. The road soon climbs to give views of the pretty valley of the little River Seven. After the Blacksmith's Arms Hotel the road reaches Cropton Forest, which is glorious with rhododendrons in early summer. Care is needed here, any time of the year, as there is a large population of deer in the surrounding woodland.

Pass the entrance to Spiers House camping site on the left. About 1 mile further on, 5 miles from Rosedale, look for a turning to the right  to Lastingham and Kirkbymoorside – this comes just before a bridge. Turn on to this road which twists down to cross a humpbacked bridge over the River Seven, now a more substantial stream. Take the main road to the right after the bridge following the signs towards Lastingham and Hutton. At Lastingham turn to the left, immediately before the church, to head for Appleton-le-Moors.

There is a fine Victorian church in Appleton (by Pearson, the architect who sympathetically restored St Mary's at Lastingham) and a broad street lined with attractive old cottages. This is an example of one of the earliest planned villages. The sites of its houses follow a plan outlined in a medieval document. **After the village the road crosses open moorland before meeting the A170. Turn right here to return to Kirkbymoorside.** ■

The wonderful Norman crypt at Lastingham

WAKEFIELD, WOOLLEY EDGE, HOLMFIRTH AND THE SUMMER WINE COUNTRY

64 MILES – 3 HOURS
START AND FINISH AT WAKEFIELD

The route starts from Wakefield, a city whose roots lie in the woollen trade established here in medieval times. Only the cathedral and the ancient chantry chapel on the nine-arched Old Bridge survive to remind us of its medieval prosperity. There are many fine Georgian houses, once occupied by mill-owners and the proprietors of the coal mines. The mines have gone now and the land has been reclaimed, as you can see as you drive along Woolley Edge. Later the route goes over the moors to Holmfirth, the home of Cleggy, Compo and Nora Batty.

Leave Wakefield on the A638 signposted to Doncaster and Pontefract. When the road forks, just after the turning to Crofton, take the A638 to the right signposted to Doncaster and The South.

Pass through the hamlet of Foulby and cross a bridge over a lake. This is part of the landscaped grounds of Nostell Park. **Just after the lake the B6273 goes off to the right. The entrance to Nostell Priory A is on the left, a few yards beyond this junction and about 5 miles from Wakefield.**

If you do not intend to visit the priory take the B6273 signposted towards Hemsworth Water Park. Then turn right, almost immediately, to Ryhill and Wintersett, passing a brickworks to the right. Cross a railway bridge and then take the first turning to the right down an unsignposted byway. Cross a disused railway and negotiate two sharp bends. Turn left at the T-junction.

Keep straight on past the driveway to the Anglers' Country Park. The road climbs a small hill and, after this, you can see Wintersett Reservoir ahead. There are a few places to park on the banks of the reservoir to enjoy the watery scenery and wildlife.

At a junction turn right, away from the village of Ryhill, on to a twisting road which is crossed by several public footpaths. There are wide views of the open countryside, much of it reclaimed from former mining activity.

Go through the hamlet of Cold Hiendley to come to a major road. Turn left and then take the first right, which is signposted to Notton and Woolley. This road comes out at the Oliver Twist Inn, on the B6132. Go straight over here and pass through the village of Notton. At the end of the village take the byway left, Keeper Lane, which dips down steeply from the main road. This is a delightfully quiet way through fields, and there are plenty of places to picnic on the wide verges. **At the A61 turn left and, after 50 yards (46 m), turn right off the main road past an official picnic place to the left (Darton Quarry) B.**

Turn right at the next crossroads and climb up towards Woolley Edge. There

Holmfirth - a beautiful town made famous by a television series

are grand views to the left over ground cleared of mining debris. **Go over a crossroads** – the road to the left descends to join with the motorway. A little further on there is the Woolley Edge viewpoint, giving a wonderful view westwards towards the Pennines. **At the second crossroads turn left to descend the bank and cross the M1 close to the Woolley Edge Services. Turn left at a T-junction to West Bretton and then fork left into the village to meet the A637.**

If you wish to visit the **Yorkshire Sculpture Park** in Bretton Country Park, turn left and then almost immediately right, at the war memorial **C**.

Otherwise, turn right on to the main road to reach a large roundabout and take the first exit, the A636 signposted to Denby Dale. There are good views from this main road, with the unusual television tower on Emley Moor prominent.

Go past the 'Welcome to Kirklees' sign and a turn to

• *PLACES OF INTEREST* •

Wakefield

When Leland visited Wakefield in 1535 he found it 'a very quik market toune' with its whole profit coming from coarse drapery. The cathedral reflects the prosperity of the town in medieval times (it was begun c.1420, rebuilt by Sir George Gilbert Scott in 1858, and promoted to cathedral status in 1888). Its spire, at 247 feet (75 m), is the highest in Yorkshire.

The Bridge Chapel is one of only four similar chantry chapels in England. It is on the bridge which spans the River Calder and dates from c. 1350.

Wakefield was the centre of the clothing trade in Yorkshire until the invention of the power loom saw the rise of Bradford early in the nineteenth century. Many fine Georgian houses grace the town, a legacy of the time when its woollen trade was thriving. It used to be the county town of the West Riding. Today its Ridings Shopping Centre is

acclaimed as one of the best in the region.

The city's museum contains some of the most bizarre exhibits to be found in any museum. These are the strange animals created by Charles Waterton in the nineteenth century. He was an explorer and collector of animals and kept a zoo at his home at Walton Hall (now a hotel). Using his skills of taxidermy, he grafted together parts of animals to make amazing creatures which were designed to illustrate religious or political characters.

Wakefield Museum, Wood Street. Open all year Mondays– Saturdays 10.30–5. Sunday 2.30–5. Telephone: (01924) 295350 or 375402.

Wakefield Art Gallery, Wentworth Terrace. Important collection of twentieth-century paintings and sculpture, including works by Hepworth and Moore. Open all year Mondays–Saturdays 10.30–5. Sundays 2.30–5. Telephone: (01924) 375402.

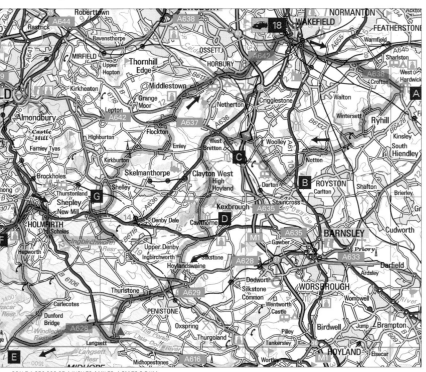

SCALE 1:250 000 OR 1 INCH TO 4 MILES *1 CM TO 2.5 KM*

Nostell Priory

Nothing remains of the original Augustinian priory founded c. 1110. The magnificent Georgian mansion was built for the Winn family who commissioned James Paine as architect in 1733 and then, twenty years later, Robert Adam, who added and decorated a further wing. The priory is the home of Lord and Lady St Oswald and is administered by the National Trust. It contains Chippendale furniture made specially for the house (Thomas Chippendale served his apprenticeship as a carpenter here) as well as tapestries and notable paintings. There is extensive parkland with three lakes and formal gardens. Wragby church is situated within the park close to the site of the original priory. It is notable for its Swiss glass, dating from 1514 to 1751.

Open Saturdays Easter–October noon–5. Also Sundays in July and August (and Summer Bank Holiday Mondays) 11–5. Telephone: (01924) 863892.

Yorkshire Sculpture Park

The beautiful parkland surrounding Bretton Hall is the setting for an outstanding exhibition of contemporary sculpture. This is particularly appropriate, since Barbara Hepworth was a native of Wakefield and Henry Moore hailed from neighbouring

Castleford. Their work features prominently in the permanent collection and there are also changing exhibitions devoted to

other sculptors working in Britain today. Entry is free.

Open in summer daily 10–6, winter 10–5. Telephone: (01924) 830579.

Yorkshire Mining Museum

The Caphouse Colliery, which belonged to the Beaumonts of Bretton Hall, was last worked in 1986 after nearly two centuries of active life. It has recently been re-opened as a museum, illustrating the history of coal mining in Yorkshire. Visitors can see the galleries where men toiled in days gone by and the machinery they used. The museum is on the Yorkshire Mining Heritage Trail, a tour which includes sixteen interesting venues (leaflet available from TICs).

Open daily throughout the year (except Christmas and New Year) 10–5. Telephone: (01924) 848806.

Cannon Hall Museum and Country Park

The hall was the home of the Spencer-Stanhope family who were involved in the industrialisation of this part of Yorkshire. They invested in coal mines, nail-making and other manufactures in the eighteenth century. Cannon Hall is now a country house museum containing furniture, glassware and a notable collection of paintings. It incorprates the regimental museum of the 13th/18th Royal Hussars.

There is an open farm in the extensive park which surrounds the mansion.

Open Tuesdays–Saturdays 10.30–5. Sundays 2.30–5. Telephone: (01226) 790270.

Holmfirth

This is a major location for the *Last of the Summer Wine* television series. It is also famous for being the home of Bamforths, the producers of saucy postcards and the makers of early movies.

The Postcard Museum, Huddersfield Road. There are displays of delightful postcards, some of them a hundred years old, and regular screenings of lantern slides and old movies. Open daily.

Last of the Summer Wine Museum, Huddersfield Road. A small museum devoted to the television series.

Emley on the right, and then **take the first turning to the left which is unsignposted except to a picnic place.** There are beautiful views as the lane drops down a hill to cross a stream running into the park at Bretton. This is the infant River Dearne which later flows through Barnsley, and is followed by a waymarked footpath which takes its name from the Dearne. Just after this, as you climb the hill, there is a picnic place to the left. The road then enters woods, passing a 'Welcome to Barnsley' sign. The lane goes by the isolated

church at High Hoyland and then comes to the village itself. **After the Cherry Tree pub fork left towards Cannon Hall Country Park.**

There are inviting footpaths on the right going through Deffer Woods. The liberal use of double yellow lines which follows shows that you are approaching the country park. There is a large car park adjacent to the lake and the park has museums, formal gardens and an open farm **D**. **Beyond the park the lane reaches the A635. Turn right and then take the first left to**

Penistone. This high road gives wide-ranging views over the countryside. **Turn right on to the A629 and then take the first left to go down Wellhouse Lane into Penistone. The lane meets the A628 at the bottom where you turn right and cross the bridge.**

If you wish to visit the town turn left at the traffic lights which follow. The church dates from the thirteenth century and the cloth hall, from where the hand-weavers of the district sold their pieces of cloth, was built in 1768.

The route continues by turning right at the traffic lights, keeping on the A628 towards Manchester. Go through Thurlstone and the adjoining village of Millhouse Green. A road to Holmfirth goes off to the right but the route continues on the A628. It crosses the River Don and then climbs steadily giving beautiful views.

When the main road turns sharply to the right, keep straight on to Langsett. As the road drops down past Moorview Farm there are wonderful views of the Langsett Reservoir and the moors surrounding it. Turn right at the bottom on to the A616. There is a picnic site almost immediately on the left.

At the crossroads turn left towards Manchester, on the A628, and enter the Peak District National Park. The road climbs steadily and the views become vast after the summit. When the main road swings round to the left take the turn to the right to Dunford Bridge . The moorland here bears the sinister name of Gallows Moss. There are further beautiful views as the little road descends with the Winscar Reservoir to the left. There is a picnic site just before you reach Dunford Bridge. Turn left after the bridge towards Holmfirth and Huddersfield. There is parking by the Winscar Reservoir with its sheer rocky sides. Keep straight on towards Holmfirth to meet the B6106 and follow this road down into the town .

Take the A635 out of Holmfirth towards Barnsley. Thongsbridge is a picturesque village. A road leads to it from the left. Continue to New Mill and bear right on to the A616 to Glossop. Pass a turn to the right which goes to Jackson Bridge. The White Horse pub made famous by Foggy, Compo and Clegg can be found here. After the Red Lion turn left up

the lane called South View. Turn left after 100 yards (91 m) to climb this steep, narrow road, which twists and turns, and bear right when it divides. The lane continues to climb with a wood to the left and wonderful views of the Holme valley to the right. There is a seat and a parking place at the top. A footpath crosses the road which links up with the Holme Valley Circular Walk.

A little further on Intake Lane goes off to the left, a dead end. Soon after this fork left onto Windmill Lane. This road appropriately heads towards a wind farm. Keep straight on along this road, going over two crossroads, the first of which bears no warning sign, to reach the A629. Turn left here and keep on this road after the A635 Barnsley to Holmfirth road crosses it. About 100 yards (91 m) after this crossroads take the road

to the right – Carr Lane . The lane leads into the village of Shelley where you briefly join the B6116 before bearing left on to Bark House Lane. This road leads to Flockton, where the church is passed to the right. This road also passes the television tower where there is a car park allowing you to enjoy a grand view.

The next village, Emley, has a medieval church and the remains of an old cross opposite the post office. Turn left here to head towards Flockton. Turn right on to the A637 at Flockton, pass the George and Dragon pub and turn left on to the road signposted to the Yorkshire Mining Museum. At the Black Swan turn left down Green Lane. This short lane soon meets with the A642 where you turn left to visit the Mining Museum or right to return to Wakefield after about 6 miles. ■

The spire of Wakefield Cathedral is the tallest in Yorkshire

SCARBOROUGH TO FLAMBOROUGH HEAD RETURNING OVER THE WOLDS

58 MILES – 2½ HOURS
START AND FINISH AT SCARBOROUGH

There is a pleasant mix of seaside, country and historical places in this tour. There are opportunities to visit Filey and Bridlington, resorts of differing character, as well as this country's only mainland gannetry and a stately home containing an outstanding collection of French paintings. Take time, if the weather permits, to stroll on the cliffs at Flamborough and then linger amidst the scenery of the Wolds to see the innumerable reminders of the people who lived here in prehistoric times – the amazing Rudston megalith, which you will visit on this tour, is but one example.

From the centre of Scarborough take the road to Filey (initially the A165 towards Bridlington). The road crosses The Ravine and then runs parallel to the South Cliff.

If you wish to see fine views of the coastline turn left, after passing a group of shops, into Esplanade Gardens. This will take you to a road following the clifftop. When the road starts to head inland return to the main road.

The route runs close to the cliffs at Cayton Bay where there is a picnic site and car park as well as a big holiday camp complex. **Keep on towards Filey and Bridlington when the B1261 joins at a roundabout. Carry straight over the next roundabout, and then turn left at the third into Filey. At the fourth roundabout keep on towards the beach.**

Almost immediately after the roundabout you will see a sign to the left pointing to a car park at the North Cliff Country Park. This is a very pleasant grassy car park, which is excellent for exploring Filey Brigg (the rocky ledge which projects ¼ mile seawards) or for visiting St Oswald's Church,

• PLACES OF INTEREST •

Scarborough
The east coast resort might have remained a sleepy fishing village but for a Mrs Farrow who discovered the medicinal qualities of a spring at Scarborough in the seventeenth century. The qualities of this water, coupled with the fashion for sea-bathing in the early nineteenth century, was the foundation of the town's success as a resort which came to fruition with the coming of the railway about fifty years later.

Scarborough has much to offer the modern visitor. There are all the usual man-made amenities one would expect to find at a modern resort set about two bays. Both have fine

expanses of sand. The harbour, overlooked by the ruins of the castle which has seen some of the bloodiest incidents of English history, is busy and colourful. Its shellfish stalls are deservedly popular with connoisseurs of whelks and winkles, while other stalls offer other locally-caught delicacies like kippers and cod.

Scarborough Castle. Round-head artillery brought down much of the masonry, but the great rectangular keep is a memorable feature of the town, standing on a headland overlooking the harbour. A Roman signal station occupied the site before the coming of the Normans. Open April–September

daily 10–6. October–March Wednesdays–Sundays 10–4. Telephone: (01723) 372451.

Scarborough Millennium, Sandside. The sights, sounds and smells of Scarborough's history. Open May–September daily 10–10. October–April daily 10–5. Telephone: (01723) 501000.

Scarborough Art Gallery, The Crescent. The actor Charles Laughton was a native of the town and bequeathed his collection of portraits and narrative paintings to it. These are housed in an elegant Italianate villa.

Open all year Tuesdays–Saturdays 10–1, 2–5 and also Sundays in summer 2–5. Telephone: (01723) 374753.

a very fine building dating from the latter part of the Norman period. In 1934 two coastguards reported seeing a 28-foot- (8.5 m) long sea monster off the Brigg which reared up in front of them and must have been 8 feet (2.4 m) high.

Continue down Church Cliff Drive passing below the church and then go beneath the fine cast-iron bridge which spans Church Ravine to reach the Coble Landing. Here the fishing-boats (cobles) are drawn up, and there are stalls selling shellfish etc. **The road bears right and climbs to the Crescent.** The fine white-painted blocks of houses give the resort a hint of the flavour of Brighton or Eastbourne.

Scarborough's south bay from above the Spa

87

Gracious buildings overlook the shore at Filey

At the Crescent turn left and then follow the signs to Bridlington. These will take you out of town past the station. The A1039 soon joins with the A165. About 3¹/₂ miles after this junction, just after Reighton, turn left off the main road at The Dotterel Inn  on to the B1229 towards Flamborough. A sign indicates that you are now in the historic 'East Riding' of Yorkshire.

The road passes through the villages of Buckton (where Hoddy Cow's Lane is at the entrance to the village on the right) and the adjoining village of Bempton, where a road to the left goes to the RSPB Bempton Cliffs Reserve. This is the only mainland nesting-site of gannets in England, and other species to breed here are guillemot, razorbills, kittiwakes and puffins. The seabirds are best seen in the nesting season from May until July, though care must be taken since the cliffs reach heights of 400 feet (122 m).

Keep on the main road to reach Flamborough **B**, turning left to reach the centre of the village facing the post office. The red granite memorial commemorates a tragedy in 1909 when the crews of two cobles perished – those on the *Two Brothers* attempting to rescue the crew of the *Gleaner*.

Here there is a choice of routes leading to car parks all of which are good starting points for coastal walks. **To visit North Landing turn left on to the B1255, and to visit Flamborough Head turn right along the B1259.** The latter takes you past the remarkable lighthouse built by John Matson in 1805 – during its construction no scaffolding was used. **If you turn south off the B1259 you can continue to the South Landing where the Heritage Centre is situated.**

From each of these cul-de-sacs you have to return to Flamborough village. If you are interested in churches, pause to visit the parish church dedicated to St Oswald, patron saint of seamen. It dates from Norman times, but is remarkable for its medieval rood-screen, the work of William Brownfleet of Ripon. It also has the macabre tomb of Sir Marmaduke Constable who died in 1520 from an unusual accident. He swallowed a toad, and this was said to have eaten his heart, a prognosis graphically illustrated on his tomb.

Turn westwards towards Bridlington on the B1255. Pass a parking area and picnic site to the left, on Danes Dyke. The earthwork originally rose to a height of 18 feet (5.5 m) with a ditch 60 feet (18.2 m) wide, and was put up across the peninsular in the Iron Age. The ditch is on the inland side, and it is suggested that it was an anti-chariot device. Is this the original last ditch? There is a woodland trail which starts from the car park, and you can also walk along the coast in either direction from here.

At Marton, where the road to Bridlington turns sharply right, turn left to pass the entrance to Sewerby Hall. The mansion was built between 1714 and 1720 by John Greame, though there were additions in the early nineteenth century. It now serves Bridlington as a museum. There is a room dedicated to the aviation pioneer, Amy Johnson, whose

Burton Agnes Hall, an outstanding Jacobean building

father gave the town her trophies and memorabilia. The gardens and park are also attractive and there is a small zoo.

Carry on through Sewerby village, pass the Bridlington model village and the clifftop car park and so come into Bridlington itself.

Take the A166 (York road) out of the town and go through the village of Carnaby. There is a pottery here as well as hotels and pubs. **Continue to Burton Agnes** C. As you approach the village the hall can be seen at the end of an avenue of beech trees. Parking for the house and church is to the right.

The route continues a little further along the main road to a turning to the right opposite the Blue Bell Inn signposted to Rudston. Keep on the major road when this lane divides. About 2 miles from Burton Agnes turn right and then, after about 200 yards (183 m), turn left still heading for Rudston. You will cross the Roman road which ran from their signal station of Flamborough Head to York.

At Rudston go through the village and then turn right on to the B1253. You will see the church ahead, but the route continues by turning left off the main road on to a lane signposted to Burton Fleming and Hunmanby. At 25¹/₂ feet (7.8 m) high, the famous monolith in Rudston churchyard is the tallest standing stone in England. The stone is gritstone, and the nearest outcrop of this is at Cayton Bay, 10 miles distant – a long way to drag a forty-ton rock. It is said that as much is buried beneath the ground as appears above it, and that the devil hurled the stone at the church when he saw it being built. Either because his aim was poor, or by divine intervention, the stone fell short!

Keep straight on when a turn to the right goes off to Grindale. At Burton Fleming turn left on to a major road into the village and keep straight on past the Burton Arms to Wold Newton. Just over 1 mile from the village the road bends sharply right to cross a bridge. On the left-hand side of the lane is a small hillock called Willy Howe, the remains of a large Neolithic long barrow. It used to be feared as a haunt of fairies.

Wold Newton has the usual spacious green with a pond in the middle. **Turn right at the centre of the village to Fordon and Flixton.** The Gypsey Race, an erratically flowing spring, rises near the village. If the stream flows swiftly it is believed that disaster will follow – the waters were abundant just before the Plague struck in 1666 and before the outbreak of both World Wars.

After Wold Newton the road climbs steadily to the top of the wolds and then abruptly dips into Fordon D, little more than a couple of farms and cottages, snug in its hidden valley. Look out for the tiny St James' Church on the left as you descend the steep hill into the hamlet. The church dates from Norman times.

At the crossroads at Fordon turn left to Willerby Wold. The road twists and turns along the crest of the hill and becomes quite narrow, even though the verges are broad. **When it meets the B1249 turn right to Scarborough.** Within about 1 mile you come to Staxton Hill Picnic Site from which there is a famous view northwards to the coastline at Scarborough. **A steep descent takes you down to the A64. Turn right to follow this road back to Scarborough.** ∎

• PLACES OF INTEREST •

Bridlington
As well as being a popular seaside resort Bridlington also has a quieter, more ancient face. The Augustinian priory was founded in 1115, and parts of it were incorporated into the magnificent parish church. As at Beverley and York, there are twin towers, though at Bridlington they do not match. The first tourists to come to Bridlington were pilgrims attracted to the priory by the shrine of St John of Bridlington dedicated to a fourteenth-century prior who lived a particularly holy life. The town became very dependent on its fishing industry after the dissolution of its priory, and has spent considerable money over the centuries in protecting the harbour and coastline from North Sea storms. It is fortunate that a freshwater spring flows from the harbour and thus keeps it free from silt.
Sewerby Hall and Park. Museum, art gallery, zoo and café. Park open daily dawn–dusk. Hall open March–September daily 10–5.30. October–February Saturdays–Tuesdays 11–4.

Telephone: (01262) 673769 or 401392.

Burton Agnes
The house is one of the finest examples of Jacobean architecture. It was designed by Robert Smithson, Master Mason to Queen Elizabeth I and architect of Longleat, Wollaton and Hardwick, for Sir Henry Griffith who died in 1620. He was descended from Roger de Stuteville who built the neighbouring Norman manor house in 1173. This was later clad in brick and roofed to serve the mansion as its laundry. The magnificent Norman undercroft survives, and the building is in the care of English Heritage and should be visited with the hall. Burton Agnes itself is a treasure-house, both architecturally and on account of the paintings, furniture and china that it contains.
Burton Agnes Manor House (English Heritage). Open all year daily. Admission free.
Burton Agnes Hall. Open April–October daily 11–5. Telephone: (01262) 490324.

KETTLEWELL, HAWES AND BISHOPDALE

60 MILES – 2½ HOURS
START AND FINISH AT KETTLEWELL

The tour begins in Upper Wharfedale and goes on to visit six more dales. The route passes through some of the finest scenery in the area, though it is recommended that you leave the car and take to the footpaths to make the most of this glorious countryside. Although the gradients are steep at times, there is nothing here that should strike fear into the motorist, unless he or she suffers from vertigo, in which case do not look to the left when climbing out of Arncliffe!

Cross the bridge taking the B1610 (Skipton road) out of Kettlewell. The spectacular Kilnsey Crag can be seen ahead, its overhang becoming more apparent the closer you get. It is a testament to the power of the Ice Age glaciers which did so much to form the landscape of the Dales. **Take the lane to the right, just before Skirfare Bridge A, a single-track road unsuitable for caravans.** The river can be quite formidable after rain, but usually it is a tranquil little stream providing a fine foreground to the views over the heather-covered moors.

Continue towards Arncliffe and ignore the turning to the left across the river at Hawkswick. The rocky crags of the limestone escarpment are spectacular as the road approaches Arncliffe. **Turn left to cross the bridge here. Pass the church on the left to reach the centre of the village and then turn right towards Malham.** There are gates across this road, though sometimes these are left open.

The road climbs out of Littondale onto the flanks of Darnbrook Fell, and the land falls precipitously on the left down to the Cowside Beck far below. There are impressive scree slopes and massive outcrops of bare rock. About 2½ miles from Arncliffe the road begins a steep descent to cross Darnbrook Beck, and then climbs to a level plateau where there are plenty of parking and picnic places. Walks lead to

Hawthorn blossom at Kettlewell in Wharfedale

part of the Pennine Way which crosses this road 2 miles or so after Darnbrook Beck. The path northwards crosses Fountains Fell and passes close to a remote tarn at the top.

The road passes a drive to the Malham Tarn Field Centre on the left. There is a parking place on the right just after this, which is useful should you wish to take the nature trail along the northern shore of the tarn. Malham Tarn stands 1,229 feet (375 m) above sea-level, which makes it the highest Pennine lake. It is noted for its plump trout, perhaps descendants of the ones caught by monks of Fountains Abbey who were given the fishery by William de Percy in the twelfth century.

Where the road divides B bear right towards Settle. If you wish to visit the southern or eastern side of Malham Tarn, the Cove, or Malham village itself bear

left. As the road climbs up to the crest of the hill wonderful views unfold to the west, with the distinctive flat top of Ingleborough obvious in the distance, and a wonderful array of more jagged hills scattered about the landscape nearer to Settle. If the day is clear you

can see the summits of the Lake District mountains from here.

At the next junction, which follows in less than 1 mile, bear right to Stainforth. Now, as the road descends, you can also see the unmistakable whale-backed form of Pen-y-ghent close to the right. **At a**

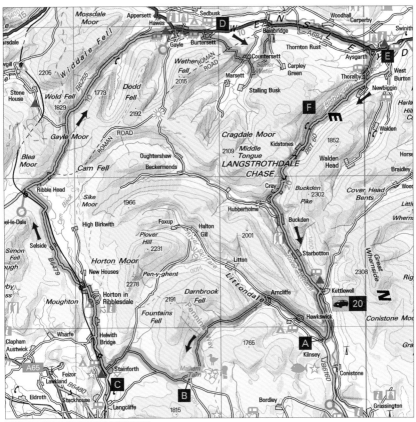

SCALE 1:250 000 OR 1 INCH TO 4 MILES *1 CM TO 2.5 KM*

T-junction turn left on to a road which descends steeply into Ribblesdale with Stainforth set amidst the trees at the bottom. Turn right towards the B6479 when the lane reaches the village. There is a car park on the left where this lane joins the B6479. **Turn right here C towards Horton in Ribblesdale.**

Great quarries dominate the landscape to the left as you approach Horton, which has a medieval church as well as a car park with toilets. The village suffered badly from plague in 1597 when seventy-four inhabitants died, an eighth of the population. Beyond Horton the road passes through attractive countryside with the railway line and the River Ribble close at hand. After Selside the road narrows – note the old railway sign on the wall of a cottage.

After 5 miles the road reaches the B6255 at Ribblehead. Turn right to Hawes. Before turning look left for a view of the famous Ribblehead viaduct, a favourite venue for those who enjoy the spectacle of a steam train climbing over the Pennines. The road runs across barren and featureless moorland compared with that seen before. But, after crossing into Richmondshire, the view begins to open up ahead and the road descends into Widdale.

Almost imperceptibly the scenery becomes pastoral. There is a stopping place for coffee just before a lane goes off to Appersett, and, quite suddenly, the view down into Wensleydale is revealed.

Join the A684 and continue on this road straight through the market town of Hawes, heading towards Aysgarth and Leyburn. Pass the Dales Countryside Museum on the left. Ignore the turning to Gayle on the right and then, $^1/2$ mile further on, turn right D to Burtersett. The lane climbs steeply into the delightful little village.

Beyond the village there are even better views down into Wensleydale. **Bear right when the road divides towards Semer Water.** After this the road climbs up very steadily, and there are magnificent views. The road turns the shoulder of the hill to give another view ahead over Raydale and then descends steeply towards Semer Water.

At Countersett turn right, and then sharp left to descend a very steep hill to a bridge and thus reach a parking place by Semer Water. This is a very popular venue with fishermen as well as being one of the highlights of the scenery of the Dales. It is said that a drowned village lies beneath the surface of the lake and that the bells of its church are sometimes heard to chime.

Continue up the steep road on the other side of the lake and, at the top, turn sharply to the left to head towards Bainbridge. There are wonderful views from this little road as it twists along the side of the valley of the River Bain before dropping dramatically

---

• *PLACES OF INTEREST* •

Arncliffe

The village, which is especially attractive in early summer when fresh leaves are on the trees and its broad green is covered in buttercups, was visited by Charles Kingsley when he was writing *The Water Babies*. He stayed at Bridge End, the old house by the bridge, and used village locations in his story. Tom met the Water Babies beneath the bridge over the Skirfare near the church.

Only the tower survives of Arncliffe's fifteenth-century church, the rest of the building having been rebuilt in 1796 in what was described as being in 'churchwarden Gothic' style. Fortunately, this dull building was itself drastically altered in 1840 and transformed into the unpretentious little church we see today.

Visitors will find many fascinating details illustrating the history of one of the largest and most remote parishes in England. There is a list of the men from the district who fought with Henry Clifford ('The Shepherd Lord' celebrated in Wordsworth's *White Doe of Rylstone*) at Flodden Field in 1513, and a pike that may have been used on that occasion hangs on the wall close by.

Malham Cove and Tarn

Some of the most sensational limestone country to be seen in England lies just to the north of Malham. The only way of seeing this is on foot, and if you leave your car in the large car park in the village, or at either of the car parks close to the tarn, you can then enjoy a wonderful 6$^1/2$-mile walk. This takes you by way of Gordale Scar with its lovely waterfall, Janet Foss, along the edge of a limestone pavement to the tarn.

The way back (assuming you have started from Malham village) takes you to the top of the 220-foot- (67 m) high cliff above Malham Cove where there is another limestone pavement scored with grikes – treacherous crevices made by thousands of years of water erosion. The path continues to the base of the natural amphitheatre, and you can then return by the beck to the village.

Semer Water

The largest natural lake in Yorkshire, covering about ninety acres, Semer Water is a puddle compared to what it was in post-Glacial times when it extended over much of Raydale. In high summer it is a busy place popular with wind-surfers, water-skiers and picnickers. At other times it is left to anglers, bird-watchers and the ghosts of the people who lived in crannogs here in prehistoric times (artificial islands made of wood and reeds on which huts were built).

down to the main road. There are remains of a Roman fort opposite this junction which guarded Wensleydale and was known as Virosidum. **Turn right on to the A684.**

After the village of Worton there is a good view of the historic Nappa Hall on the left – nestling beneath a limestone crag. The ghost of Mary Queen of Scots is supposed to haunt the medieval pele tower. She was friendly with the Metcalfe family, its owners, and persuaded her captors to allow her to visit them while she was held prisoner at Bolton Castle. **At Aysgarth pass the George and Dragon Inn and then turn right ▣ by a garage to Thoralby.** There is a lovely view as the road descends steeply into Bishopdale. Thoralby is another attractive Dales village with a broad green. It was once famous for providing hand-stitched boots. Bishopdale is notable for its fine seventeenth-century farmhouses. The tenant farmers became yeomen earlier here than elsewhere in the Dales and were thus able to buy their own farms.

Follow the signs to Kettlewell and Skipton to cross a small bridge and then bear right for Kettlewell. This brings you to the B6160 where you bear right. A little further on there is a farmhouse tearoom on the left.

Be ready for a very sharp turn ▣ when the road bends suddenly to cross a small bridge. After this it is more enclosed and much narrower. The road climbs steadily to reach the summit of the Kidstones Pass at 1,392 feet (424 m) going beneath Kidstone Scar, a spectacular outcrop of limestone to the right. You will see National Trust signs saying that this is part of their Upper Wharfedale property. The road then dips down into Wharfedale.

The village of Cray (its name derives from a word meaning fresh, clear water) marks the

The parish church at Horton-in-Ribblesdale with Pen-y-ghent in the distance

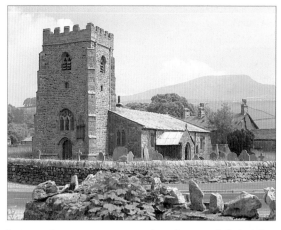

beginning of a picturesque section as the road follows the wooded dale. There are wonderful views to the right and several parking places in old quarries.

The next village is Buckden, where there is a car park. Buckden's name clearly reflects its origins as a place connected with hunting. In medieval times the foresters protecting Langstrothdale Chase for the Percy family made the first settlement here. Buckden Pike, immediately to the north east of the village, is one of the most formidable summits of the Dales, rising to a height of 2,303 feet

(702 m). Its great bulk divided the glacier flowing down Langstrothdale and thus made Upper Wharfedale and Bishopdale into U-shaped valleys typical of glaciated scenery.

Starbotton is the next village, 2½ miles southwards. The lead workings on Cam Head are probably the main reason for there being a settlement here, though in 1686 the village was virtually wiped out when Cam Gill, the innocuous-looking little stream which flows into the village from the north, swept away nearly all of its houses. **Starbotton is the last village before Kettlewell comes into view.** ■

An excellent footpath leads to Malham Cove from the village

USEFUL ADDRESSES AND INFORMATION

For information on daily events and weather forecasts

BBC Radio Cleveland 95.00 FM
BBC Radio Humberside
95.9 FM 1485kh AM
BBC Radio Leeds 92.4 FM 774kh AM
BBC Radio York
95.5, 103.7, 104.3FM 666kh AM
North York Moors Weather Forecast
Tel: (0891) 500400

Market Days
Mondays
Pickering, Thirsk, Hellifield, Skipton
Tuesdays
Bedale, Hawes, Settle
Wednesdays
Kirkbymoorside, Northallerton, Masham, Skipton
Thurdays
Guisborough, Richmond (indoor)
Fridays
Helmsley, Stokesley, Ingleton, Leyburn, Skipton
Saturdays
Guisborough, Malton, Northallerton, Thirsk,Whitby, Richmond, Skipton

National Park Information Centres
Yorkshire Dales
Aysgarth Falls Tel: (01969) 663424
Clapham Tel: (015242) 51419
Grassington Tel: (01756) 752774
Hawes Tel: (01969) 667450
Malham Tel: (01729)830363
Sedbergh Tel: (015396) 20125
North York Moors
The Moors Centre
Danby Tel: (01287) 660654
Sutton Bank Visitor Centre
Tel: (01845) 597426
Information Helpline
Tel: (0891) 664342

National Trust Regional Office
The National Trust, Goddards,
27 Tadcaster Road, Dringhouses,
York YO2 2QG
Tel: (01904) 702021

Tourist Information Centres
Opening times vary – check by phone
Bedale
Bedale Hall, Bedale, North Yorkshire
DL8 1AA. Tel: (01677) 424604
Beverley
The Guildhall, Register Square,
Beverley, Humberside HU17 9AU
Tel: (01482) 867430/883898
Bridlington
25 Prince Street, Bridlington,
Humberside YO15 2NP
Tel: (01262) 673474/606383

Danby
The Moors Centre, Danby Lodge,
Lodge Lane, Danby, Whitby,
North Yorkshire YO21 2NB
Tel: (01287) 660654
Filey
John Street, Filey, North Yorkshire
YO14 9DW. Tel: (01723) 512204
Grassington
National Park Centre, Hebden Road,
North Yorkshire BD23 5LB
Tel: (01756) 752774
Great Ayton
High Green Car Park, Great Ayton,
Middlesborough, Cleveland TS9 6BJ
Tel: (01642) 722835
Guisborough
Fountain Street, Guisborough, Cleveland
TS14 6QF. Tel: (01287) 633801
Harrogate
Royal Baths Assembly Rooms, Crescent
Road, Harrogate, North Yorkshire
HG1 2RR. Tel: (01423) 525666
Hawes
Dales Coutryside Museum, Station Yard,
Hawes, North Yorkshire DL8 3NT
Tel: (01969) 667450
Haworth
2-4 West Lane, Haworth, Nr Keighley,
West Yorkshire BD22 8EF
Tel: (01535) 642329
Hebden Bridge
1 Bridge Gate, Hebden Bridge, West
Yorkshire HX7 8EX. Tel: (01422) 843831
Helmsley
Town Hall, Market Place, Helmsley, North
Yorkshire YO6 5BL. Tel: (01439) 70173
Holmfirth
49-51 Huddersfield Road,
Holmfirth, West Yorkshire HD7 1JP
Tel: (01484) 687603
Horton in Ribbledale
Pen-y-ghent Café, Horton in Ribblesdale,
Settle, North Yorkshire BD24 0HE
Tel: (01729) 860333
Humber Bridge
North Bank Viewing Area, Ferriby Road,
Hessle, Humberside HU13 0LN
Tel: (01482) 640852
Ilkley
Station Road, Ilkley, West Yorkshire
LS29 8HA. Tel: (01943) 602319
Ingleton
Community Centre Car Park,
Ingleton, North Yorkshire LA6 8HA
Tel: (015242) 41049
Knaresborough
35 Market Place, Knaresborough, North
Yorkshire HG5 8AL. Tel: (01423) 866886
Malton
The Old Town Hall, Market Place,
Malton, North Yorkshire YO17 0LH
Tel: (01653) 600048
Pateley Bridge
14 High Street, Pateley Bridge,
North Yorkshire HG3 5AW
Tel: (01423) 711147

Pickering
Eastgate Car Park, Pickering, North
Yorkshire YO18 7DP. Tel: (01751) 73791
Richmond
Friary Gardens, Victoria Road,
Richmond, North Yorkshire DL10 4AJ
Tel: (01748) 850252 or 825994
Ripon
Minster Road, Ripon, North Yorkshire
HG4 1LT. Tel: (01765) 604625
Scarborough
St Nicholas Cliff, Scarborough,
North Yorkshire YO11 2EP
Tel: (01723) 373333
Scotch Corner
Pavilion Service Area A1, Scotch Corner,
Nr Richmond, North Yorkshire DL10 6PQ
Tel: (01325) 377677
Settle
Town Hall, Cheapside, Settle,
North Yorkshire BD24 9EJ
Tel: (01729) 825192
Skipton
8 Victoria Square, Skipton,
North Yorkshire BD23 1JF
Tel: (01756) 792809
Sutton Bank
Sutton Bank Visitor Centre,
Nr Thirsk, North Yorkshire YO7 2EK
Tel: (01845) 597426
Thirsk
14 Kirkgate, Thirsk, North Yorkshire
YO7 1PQ. Tel: (01845) 522755
Wakefield
Town Hall, Wood Street, Wakefield,
West Yorkshire WF1 2HQ
Tel: (01924) 295000/295001
Whitby
Langborne Road, Whitby,
North Yorkshire YO21 1YN
Tel: (01947) 602674
York
De Gray Rooms, Exhibition Square,
York, North Yorkshire YO1 2HB
Tel: (01904) 621756

Other useful organisations
Council for National Parks
246 Lavender Hill, London SW11 1LJ
Tel: (0171) 9244077
Forest Enterprise,
North York Moors Forest District,
42 Eastgate, Pickering,
North Yorkshire YO18 7DU
Tel: (01751) 72711 or 73810
Forest Enterprise Information Centre
Low Dalby, Pickering
Tel: (01751) 460295
Ordnance Survey
Romsey Road, Maybush,
Southampton SO16 4GU
Tel: (01703) 792912
TIC Travel Office
6 Rougier Street, York, North Yorkshire
YO2 1JA. Tel: (01904) 620557
York Railway Station
Outer Concourse, York, North Yorkshire
YO2 2AY. Tel: (01904) 643700
Yorkshire & Humberside Tourist Board
312 Tadcaster Road, York YO2 2HF
Tel: (01904) 707961

INDEX